CONTENTS

AFGHANISTAN: LAW ENFORCEMENT INTERDICTION EFFORTS IN TRANSSHIPMENT COUNTRIES TO STEM THE FLOW OF HEROIN

THURSDAY, FEBRUARY 26, 2004

HOUSE OF REPRESENTATIVES,
SUBCOMMITTEE ON CRIMINAL JUSTICE, DRUG POLICY AND HUMAN RESOURCES,
COMMITTEE ON GOVERNMENT REFORM,
Washington, DC.

The subcommittee met, pursuant to notice, at 2:10 p.m., in room 2154, Rayburn House Office Building, Hon. Mark E. Souder (chairman of the subcommittee) presiding.

Present: Representatives Souder, Carter, Cummings, Ruppersberger, and Norton.

Staff present: J. Marc Wheat, staff director and chief counsel; John Stanton, congressional fellow; Nicole Garrett, clerk; Tony Haywood, minority counsel; and Jean Gosa, minority assistant clerk.

Mr. SOUDER. The subcommittee will come to order.

Good afternoon. I thank you all for coming. Today our subcommittee will address the problem of transshipment of the various stages of production, from poppy to opium and finally to heroin, from Afghanistan to neighboring countries and elsewhere to market.

We will learn that the estimates of hectares under cultivation are now approaching the highest level of past production. The cultivation of poppy and the production of opium under the Taliban rule reached an individual high of 4,600 metric tons in 1999.

If you glance at the United Nations Office on Drug Control and Crime chart on the easel to my left, on the far right side of that chart you can see the production estimates in the postwar on terrorism period. On the second easel you can see a 4-year comparison from 2000 to 2003, the last full year of Taliban production. Then the Taliban crackdown. And then the explosive growth during the U.S.-led war on terrorism. Needless to say, this is a very troubling trend.

A significant problem is the judicial system in Afghanistan. It does not exist, for all practical purposes. Afghanistan does not have the facilities to incarcerate convicted citizens notwithstanding any possibility of due process. The Taliban ordered farmers to stop raising poppy in 2001 and stockpiled what product there was. They enforced the ban with lethal force, not with judicial process. The farmers complied. The farmers also survived by growing other crops in the interim. Some have said that the Taliban's motive was not to rid the world of heroin but to reduce the supply of nonTaliban narcotics and significantly drive up the value of their supplies. The Karzai government and the U.S.-led coalition has not resorted to such measures to enforce a reduction or outright ban on poppy growth; therefore, there is no real penalty for growing an illegal cash crop like opium poppy.

So the question of disrupting this particular market must be focused on the regions surrounding Afghanistan and the efforts to stop the various stages of heroin production from reaching any consumer market. We will learn which routes are commonly taken, through which neighboring countries, and what is being done to interdict these shipments.

The graphic on the third easel shows what the U.N. thinks of the transshipment routes and the major trafficking hubs.

This problem is worldwide, affecting entire continents. The magnitude of the transshipment problem is reflected in the destination markets. The United Nations research on drug abuse revealed that the opiate abuse ranked first in 30 Asian countries, first in 34 Europeans countries, first in the Australian continent, and second in North America among drug users in treatment. Only Africa and South America had a minority percentage of drug users addicted and seeking treatment for opiate abuse.

I am concerned about this problem because over 20,000 Americans die every year from drugs, and 7 to 10 percent of heroin sold in the United States comes from the Afghan region.

The next issue to examine is the matter of working relationships with international and Federal law enforcement officials and agencies. Any effective interdiction efforts rely heavily on trust and shared information. The Department of State develops relationships with host nation law enforcement officials where we have embassies. The International Narcotics and Law Enforcement Affairs Bureau is establishing training relationships that seek and disburse assistance funding. Similarly, the Drug Enforcement Administration has agents assigned to many foreign countries to advise and assist host nation law enforcement officials with investigation, law enforcement technology, and training vetted units. With the consolidation of many other Federal law enforcement agencies in the new Department of Homeland Security, who passes information about a load in transit to DHS so that an interdiction can take place at sea, at ports of entry, or the areas between the ports of entry; and how is the information passed? What is the working relationship with respect to counternarcotics with the Department of Defense in Afghanistan and the surrounding region?

I have recently returned from overseas, having visited Libya, Iraq, Afghanistan, and Pakistan. I have seen some of the challenges our witnesses will discuss firsthand. I am very interested in what the solutions are, however. What assistance does the United States provide to each of the countries in the region to help detect and interdict the opium product, the precursor chemicals, and the money? I hope the witnesses will address the possibility of eradication programs within Afghanistan, the interdiction strategies by country in the region, the foreign assistance and alternative economic development plans, and specific information on resource allocation and needs to properly address this crucial and grave problem.

This hearing will address all these difficult issues as well as other legislative and other potential solutions.

We are pleased to be joined by Mr. Robert Charles of the Department of State, former staff director of this subcommittee in kind of less glorious days before he went off to the big powerful State Department, and Mrs. Karen Tandy of the Drug Enforcement Administration, who has been a wonderful new director there and has also hired the next staff director at this subcommittee to work with her. And they will both share their insights and concerns and solutions to how to address these problems. Both witnesses have been to Afghanistan and the region recently, so I expect we will engage in particularly insightful discourse.

We will be joined shortly by Ranking Member Mr. Cummings, who I will have do his opening statement if he does it at that point. And I thank everyone for taking the time to join us this afternoon and I look forward to hearing the testimony of our witnesses.

[The prepared statement of Hon. Mark E. Souder follows:]

Opening Statement
Chairman Mark Souder

"Afghanistan: Law Enforcement Interdiction Efforts in Transshipment Countries to Stem the Flow of Heroin"

Subcommittee on Criminal Justice, Drug Policy, and Human Resources
Committee on Government Reform

February 26, 2004

Good afternoon, and thank all of you for coming. Today our Subcommittee will address the problem of transshipment of the various stages of production from poppy, to opium, and finally to heroin from Afghanistan, through the neighboring countries and elsewhere to market.

We will learn that the estimates of hectares under cultivation are now approaching the highest level of past production. The cultivation of poppy and production of opium under the Taliban rule reached an individual high of 4,600 metric tons in 1999, if you'll glance at the United Nations Office on Drugs and Crime chart on the easel. On the far right side of the chart, you can see that production estimates in the post - War on Terrorism period. On the second easel, you can see a four-year comparison, from 2000 to 2003, of the last full year of Taliban production, then the Taliban crack-down, and then the explosive growth during the U.S. led War on Terrorism.

A significant problem is the judicial system in Afghanistan. It does not exist for all practical purposes. Afghanistan does not have the facilities to incarcerate convicted citizens, notwithstanding any possibility of due process. The Taliban ordered farmers to stop raising poppy in 2001 and stockpiled what product there was. They enforced the ban with lethal force, not with judicial process. The farmers complied. The farmers also survived by growing other crops, in the interim. Some have said that the Taliban's motive was not to rid the world of heroin, but to reduced the supply of non-Taliban narcotics, and significantly drive up the value of their supplis. The Karzai government and the U.S. led coalition has not resorted to such measures to enforce a reduction or outright ban on poppy growth. Therefore, there is no real penalty for growing an illegal cash crop like opium poppy.

So the question of disrupting this particular market must be focused on the region surrounding Afghanistan and the efforts to stop the various stages of heroin production from reaching any consumer market. We will learn which routes are commonly taken, through which neighboring countries, and what is being done to interdict these shipments. The graphic on the third easel shows what the UN thinks are the transshipment routes and major trafficking hubs.

This problem is worldwide, affecting entire continents. The magnitude of the transshipment problem is reflected in the destination markets. The United Nations' Research on Drug Abuse revealed that opiate abuse ranked first in 30 Asian countries, first in 34 European countries, first in the Australian continent, and second in North America, among drug users in treatment. Only Africa and South America had a minority percentage of drug users addicted and seeking treatment for opiate abuse. I am concerned about this problem because over 20,000 Americans die every year from drugs, and 7-10% of heroin sold in the U.S. comes from the Afghan region.

The next issue to examine is the matter of working relationships with international and with Federal law enforcement officials and agencies. Any effective interdiction efforts rely heavily on trust and shared information. The Department of State develops relationships with host nation law enforcement officials where we have embassies. The International Narcotics and Law Enforcement Affairs Bureau is establishing training relationships and seek and disburse assistance funding. Similarly, the Drug Enforcement Administration has agents assigned to many foreign countries to advise and assist host nation law enforcement officials with investigations, law enforcement technology, and training vetted units. With the consolidation of many other Federal law enforcement agencies into the new Department of Homeland Security, who passes information about a load in transit to DHS so that an interdiction can take place at sea, at ports of entry, or the areas between ports of entry and how is the information passed? What is the working relationship, with respect to counternarcotics, with the Department of Defense in Afghanistan and the surrounding region?

I have recently returned from overseas, having visited Libya, Iraq, Afghanistan, and Pakistan. I have seen some of the challenges our witnesses will discuss, first hand. I am very interested in what the solutions are, however. What assistance does the United States provide to each of the countries in the region to help detect and interdict the opium product, the precursor chemicals, and the money? I hope the witnesses will address:

- The possibility of eradication programs within Afghanistan,
- The interdiction strategies by country in the region,
- The foreign assistance and alternative economic development plans, and
- Specific information on resource allocation and needs to properly address this crucial and grave problem.

This hearing will address all these difficult issues, as well as legislative and other potential solutions. We are pleased to be joined by Mr. Robert Charles of the Department of State and Mrs. Karen Tandy of the Drug Enforcement Administration who will share their insights, concerns, and solutions. Both witnesses have been to the region recently, so I expect we will engage in particularly insightful discourse.

I thank everyone for taking the time to join us this afternoon, and I look forward to hearing the testimony of our witnesses.

Mr. SOUDER. Let me take care of a few procedural matters first. I ask unanimous consent that all Members have 5 legislative days to submit written statements and questions for the hearing record; that any answers to written questions provided by the witnesses also be included in the record.

Without objection, it is so ordered.

I also ask unanimous consent that all exhibits, documents, and other materials referred to by Members and the witnesses may be included in the hearing record; that all Members be permitted to revise and extend their remarks.

And, without objection, it is so ordered.

Now, as Ms. Tandy and Mr. Charles well know, it is the standard procedure in this committee to swear in the witnesses.

And, actually, before we do that, would you like to do your opening statement at this point before I——

Mr. CUMMINGS. Of course.

Mr. SOUDER. I yield to Mr. Cummings.

Mr. CUMMINGS. Thank you. Thank you very much.

Mr. Chairman, 2 years after the U.S.-led forces ousted the Taliban regime, opium production in Afghanistan has skyrocketed to record levels as farmers have dramatically increased their opium output.

Earlier this month, the United Nations Office on Drugs and Crime estimated that Afghan opium production in 2003 reached 3,600 metric tons, a 6 percent increase over previous years' estimates. The country's highest opium production level since 1999, this volume represents 75 percent of the world's illicit opium production. Afghanistan since the 1980's has been a source country for heroin consumed in the West, the Middle East, and parts of Asia. Since 2000, it has been the world's leading opium producer. Historically, 80 to 90 percent of the opium consumed in Europe has traveled the so-called Balkan route from Afghanistan to Turkey— to Iran to Turkey to the Balkan countries and finally to Europe.

Although Afghan opium accounts for only a small percentage of heroin presently being consumed in the United States, opium production in Afghanistan nevertheless has major implications for United States security interests. This fact was brought into stark relief after the September 11 terrorist attacks when Americans learned that the Taliban regime which aided and abetted al Qaeda was largely sustained by proceeds derived from the trafficking of Afghan opium. UNODC estimates that Afghanistan's 2003 opium output could be worth $2.3 billion, a figure that dwarfs the country's $40 million in official exports to neighboring Pakistan. UNODC also reports that opium poppy is being grown in 28 other countries, 32 provinces, despite the fact that opium cultivation is officially banned and carries stiff penalties under Afghan law.

Contributing to the problem are consecutive years of drought during the 1990's which reduced the amount of aeratable land in Afghanistan by 37 percent. Irrigation remains a major problem for Afghan farmers who make 38 times as much profit from opium as they can from wheat, the second most viable crop.

Because of this, further increases in production are likely in 2004, absent aggressive countermeasures. Controlled by warlords and crime cartels, the resurge in the Afghan opium trade has undermined ongoing efforts by the regime of the interim Afghan President, Hamid Karzai, to establish a strong central government, democratic rule, and a legitimate economy.

According to UNODC, Executive Director Antonio Costa, the results of the 2003 survey, in part, the unequivocal warning that illegal opium production will continue to thrive unless resolute actions are taken. Such actions, he said, must include economic assistance for farmers, eradication of opium fields, and interdiction of traffickers. Mr. Costa stressed that opium production poses a formidable threat to the future of the interim government led by President Karzai when he observed recently, "I don't think we can call it a narco-state now, but Afghanistan is at a critical juncture. It can go either way."

The more we allow the narco-economy to become ingrained in the behavior of key people, the more we allow the narco-economy to penetrate legitimate business, the more we allow military commanders to benefit and profit from these activities, the greater the risk, then, the country will go the wrong way.

UNODC believes that hundreds of millions of dollars in narcotics profits are ending up in the hands of terrorist groups, including remnants of the Taliban and al Qaeda which control shipping routes with roadblocks.

A recent U.S. Security Council mission to Afghanistan affirmed this view, citing drug trafficking alongside terrorism and factional warfare as a triple threat to the reconstruction process. In January, Afghanistan pledged more aggressive efforts to fight drug cultivation and trafficking, and the country has entered several regional cooperation agreements with neighboring countries to fight drug trafficking and terrorism. Still, it appears the flow of Afghan opium across the porous borders separating these countries continues unabated, as does the flow of drug proceeds into the hands of terrorists plotting harm against the United States and our allies.

Equating drug trafficking with terrorism, UNODC recently has called on coalition forces in Afghanistan and the North Atlantic Treaty Organization, International Security Assistance Force, to help the country fight the illicit drug trade. In addition, there is reluctance among coalition governments to involve their troops in antidrug trafficking activity because the troops immediately would become targets of the all powerful drug syndicates.

Despite this, news reports indicate that Britain and Germany have recently sent, or pledged to send, troops to fight drug trafficking in Afghanistan, and the U.S. military commanders are evaluating whether to expand the role of American troops in assisting the Afghan Government's antidrug efforts. The State Department's Bureau of International Narcotics and the Law Enforcement Affairs and the Drug Enforcement Administration play lead roles in implementing U.S. foreign policy in the area of narcotics control. The DEA has a small representation in Afghanistan and regional transshipment countries, and in 2002 launched a multinational operation containment initiative to deny market access to drug traffickers and to deny terrorist groups access to illicit proceeds from drugs, precursors, weapons, and ammunition.

Both DEA Administrator Karen Tandy and Assistant Secretary of State Robert Charles have recently returned from the Afghan capital of Kabul where they and other senior U.S. officials met with President Karzai, UNODC Executive Director Costa and other representatives from Afghan and the European Union to discuss the challenges posed by Afghan drug production.

Today's hearing provides us an opportunity to hear from these two key officials concerning what U.S. foreign policy initiatives are underway and what more must be done to curtail opium production and trafficking within Afghanistan, to keep Afghan heroin from reaching international markets, and to prevent the drug trade from fueling the vehicles of terrorism.

And so with that, Mr. Chairman, I thank you, and I look forward to the testimony.

[The prepared statement of Hon. Elijah E. Cummings follows:]

Opening Statement of

Representative Elijah E. Cummings, D-Maryland
Ranking Minority Member

Hearing on "Afghanistan: Law Enforcement Interdiction Efforts in Transshipment Countries to Stem the Flow of Heroin"

Subcommittee on Criminal Justice, Drug Policy and Human Resources
Committee on Government Reform
U.S. House of Representatives
108th Congress

February 26, 2004

Mr. Chairman,

Two years after U.S.-led forces ousted the Taliban regime, opium production in Afghanistan has skyrocketed to record levels, as farmers have dramatically increased their opium output. Earlier this month, the United Nations Office on Drugs and Crime (UNODC) estimated that Afghan opium production in 2003 reached 3,600 metric tons, a 6% increase over previous year estimates. The country's highest opium production level since 1999, this volume represents fully 75% of the world's illicit opium production.

Afghanistan, since the 1980s, has been a source country for heroin consumed in the West, the Middle East, and parts of Asia. Since 2000, it has been the world's leading opium producer. Historically, 80%-90% of the opium consumed in Europe has traveled the so-called Balkan route, from Afghanistan to Iran to Turkey to the Balkan countries, and, finally, to Europe.

Although Afghan opium accounts for only a small percentage of the heroin presently being consumed in the United States, opium production in Afghanistan nonetheless has major implications for United States security interests. This fact was brought into stark relief after the 9-11 terrorist attacks, when Americans learned that the Taliban regime, which aided and abetted Al Qaeda, was largely sustained by proceeds derived from the trafficking of Afghan opium.

UNODC estimates that Afghanistan's 2003 opium output could be worth $2.3 billion, a figure that dwarfs the country's $40 million in official exports to neighboring Pakistan. UNODC also reports that opium poppy is being grown in 28 of the country's 32 provinces, despite the fact that opium cultivation is officially banned and carries stiff penalties under Afghan law.

Contributing to the problem are consecutive years of drought during the 1990s, which reduced the amount of arable land in Afghanistan by 37%. Irrigation remains a major problem for Afghan farmers who make 38 times as much profit from opium as they can from wheat (the second most viable crop). Because of this, further increases in production are likely in 2004, absent aggressive counter-measures.

Controlled by warlords and crime cartels, the resurgent Afghan opium trade has undermined ongoing efforts by the regime of interim Afghan President Hamid Karzai to establish a strong central government, democratic rule, and a legitimate economy. According to UNODC Executive Director Antonio Maria Costa, the results of the 2003 survey "impart the unequivocal warning that illegal opium production will continue to thrive unless resolute actions are taken." Such actions, he said, must include economic assistance for farmers, eradication of opium fields and interdiction of traffickers.

Mr. Costa stressed that opium production poses a formidable threat to the future of the interim government led by President Hamid Karzai when he observed recently:

> I don't think we can call it a narco-state now but Afghanistan is at a critical juncture – it could go either way . . . The more we allow the narco-economy to become ingrained in the behavior of key people, the more we allow the narco-economy to penetrate legitimate business, the more we allow military commanders to benefit and profit from these activities, the greater the risk that the country will go the wrong way.

UNODC believes that hundreds of millions of dollars in narcotics profits are ending up in the hands of terrorist groups, including remnants of the Taliban and Al Qaeda, which control shipping routes with roadblocks. A recent United Nations Security Council mission to Afghanistan affirmed this view, citing drug trafficking alongside terrorism and factional warfare as a "triple threat" to the reconstruction process.

In January, Afghanistan pledged more aggressive efforts to fight drug cultivation and trafficking and the country has entered several regional cooperation agreements with neighboring countries to fight drug trafficking and terrorism. Still, it appears, the flow of Afghan opium across the porous borders separating these countries continues unabated, as does the flow of drug proceeds into the hands of terrorists plotting harm against the United States and our allies.

Equating drug trafficking with terrorism, UNODC recently has called on coalition forces in Afghanistan and the North Atlantic Treaty Organization-led (NATO) International Security Assistance Force (ISAF) to help the country fight the illicit drug trade. In addition, there is reluctance among coalition governments to involve their troops in anti-drug trafficking activity because the troops immediately would become targets of the all-powerful drug syndicates. Despite this, news reports indicate that Britain and Germany have recently sent or pledged to send troops to fight drug trafficking in Afghanistan, and U.S. military commanders are evaluating whether to expand the role of American troops in assisting the Afghan government's anti-drug efforts.

The State Department's Bureau of International Narcotics and Law Enforcement Affairs ("INL") and the Drug Enforcement Administration play lead roles in implementing U.S. foreign policy in the area of narcotics control. The DEA has a small representation in Afghanistan and regional transshipment countries and, in 2002, launched the multi-national "Operation Containment" initiative to deny market access to drug traffickers and to deny terrorist groups access to illicit proceeds from drugs, precursors, weapons, and ammunition.

Both DEA Administrator Karen Tandy and Assistant Secretary of State Robert Charles have recently returned from the Afghan capital of Kabul, where they and other senior U.S.

officials met with President Karzai, UNODC Executive Director Costa and other representatives from Afghanistan and the European Union to discuss the challenges posed by Afghan drug production. Today's hearing provides us an opportunity to hear from these two key officials concerning what U.S. foreign policy initiatives are underway, and what more must be done, to curtail opium production and trafficking within Afghanistan, to keep Afghan heroin from reaching international markets, and to prevent the drug trade from fueling the vehicles of terrorism.

Thank you for holding this important hearing. I look forward to hearing the testimony of our witnesses.

##

Mr. SOUDER. I want to thank the ranking member, Mr. Cummings, for his leadership on the narcotics effort. It has really been great to work on this in a bipartisan way and to make sure we are tackling it both in the United States, and before it gets to our streets here in the United States and around the world.

With that, I think we will go ahead with the swearing in of the witnesses. It's the standard practice of this subcommittee to have you testify under oath. So if each of you would stand and raise your right hands.

[Witnesses sworn.]

Mr. SOUDER. Let the record show that both responded in the affirmative. And it would be really sad if we had to go after our former staff director of this committee if he didn't tell the truth. So, you are now even more under oath than normal.

Obviously he always tells the truth. I just had to harass him just because it's his first official appearance.

With that, we will go to Mr. Robert Charles, Assistant Secretary of State for Narcotics.

STATEMENT OF ROBERT CHARLES, ASSISTANT SECRETARY, DEPARTMENT OF STATE, INTERNATIONAL NARCOTICS AND LAW ENFORCEMENT AFFAIRS

Mr. CHARLES. Thank you, Mr. Chairman. And I also want to thank both of you personally. You have been leaders in this fight and in Congress for as long as you have served, and I think in both of your parties and for Congress as a whole your leadership allows the rest of us to do our jobs. So I am just grateful that you are there and for this hearing. I also agree with both of your opening statements, and just want to add what insight we can from our perspective.

Again, I appreciate the opportunity to speak before you today on the subject of Afghanistan, the narcotics situation and strategy, the administration's strategy for dealing with narcotics, both within Afghanistan and trafficked from it, is proactive and coordinated in the interagency. It is intended to reduce measurably the heroin poppy cultivation, to encourage alternative income streams, to destroy drug labs, to promote drug interdiction, and to develop the justice sector to facilitate proper prosecution and sentencing of traffickers.

This State Department bureau, the Bureau of International Narcotics and Law Enforcement, is intent on working closely and effectively both with Congress and the DEA to implement this strategy. As you indicated, in fact the DEA administrator and I have recently returned from a fact-finding trip to Afghanistan, where we represented the U.S. Government at the Counternarcotics Conference in Kabul earlier this month.

Pieces of this counternarcotics strategy are proportionate to the urgency and to the needs presented on the ground. The various pieces of this emerging strategy are both complementary and independently important. The key words are, I think, proactive, comprehensive, and accountable.

A few first impressions, again, confirming some of the things you have said in your opening statements. My recent meeting with President Karzai reaffirmed my conviction that he means business.

He is serious about tackling the heroin threat in his country. This is a leader who is dedicated to breaking the cycle of opium poppy cultivation and narcotics trafficking in his country before local trafficking rings become cartels and put down tap roots, transforming Afghanistan into what some might call a narco-state. President Karzai is determined, I think, to proceed with every major aspect of breaking the heroin trade, even as he reinforces the productivity of alternative legitimate income streams such as through the production of wheat, maize, barley, and other needed crops.

One thing I would ask if we could take a look, one of the charts indicates how the Afghan economy really is made up. Farmers don't make much on heroin poppy. On the other hand, they do make more than they make in other crops. But I think one of the things that people fail to understand is that 98 percent of the economy is actually in legitimate crops, wheat, barley, maize, rice. And so we want to encourage that to grow.

As you know, there are three essential components to our accelerating counternarcotics strategy. The first component is targeting the eradication of the heroin poppies. The second is the targeted, ever-widening availability and reinforcement of alternative streams of income. Democracies, of course, are consolidated not by reliance on drug money, but by pairing well-supported democratic institutions and the rule of law with the sound growing in free market and legitimate goods.

Afghanistan has great needs, for example, in the area of legitimate agriculture. Food is a problem, and that is one of the reasons this strategy, I think, also works well and is intended to meet those needs. We intend to support the growth of the legitimate economy in that and other sectors.

Third, and finally, law enforcement, interdiction, and the justice sector reform are also key to success. We must raise the costs and risks of heroin trafficking while raising the incentives for joining and remaining a part of the legitimate economy. Only 8 percent, as that chart indicates, of Afghanistan's cultivated land is presently used to grow poppies, and we must make the incremental risk of associated heroin poppy profits higher than the extra income it might produce.

There are other dangers from which we cannot avert our gaze. Afghanistan's heroin, which sells on the retain market for about 100 times the farm gate price, the price that the farmer gets, is a source of a growing reservoir of illegal money that funds international crime across the region, sustains the destabilizing activities of warlords, and fosters local coercion and terrorism. While available information about this pattern continues to grow, we cannot afford to stand by and wait as these destructive relationships and behaviors become clearer and more closely institutionalized. Our comprehensive approach takes stock of these linkages and is accelerating the effort to break each of them.

A few final thoughts. On eradication, some would argue, wait. Other priorities, they suggest, might trump this activity. I would argue that swift action is essential. Distinguishing the urgent from the otherwise important requires that we tackle the poppy crop now. So we are doing that with the Afghan security, in a two-phase program led by the British initially, and after April or May, by U.S. support to the Afghan central government.

Second, I can say without qualification that we have a commited ally in the Afghanistan Government. President Karzai believes in democracy, the rule of law and human rights, and a robust counter-narcotics effort. I see no signs of half-measures, and we are similarly committed.

Third, I am convinced that the drug money in terrorist organizations in Afghanistan and throughout the region are like chain links, bound tightly by mutually reinforcing motivations and operations. While there are other links in that chain, it is my conviction, based on the information available, that these two threats overlap palpably and incontrovertibly in Afghanistan.

Fourth, we are cooperating closely with our European allies to support the Afghan Government. We are pressing for increased coordination and cooperation from the British on counternarcotics, the Germans on policing, and the Italians on justice sector reform.

Fifth, and finally, INL, the Bureau of International Narcotics and Law Enforcement, is determined to support and encourage cooperation between not only other efforts of the State Department but also DEA, DOD, and USAID. Congress empowers us to achieve these results for the American people and for the Afghan people and for the greater local, regional, and international security of all of us. Congress has funded the INL coordinated portion of this effort with 50 million in supplemental appropriations in fiscal year 2004, of which a significant portion is dedicated to eradication.

Separately, you have funded INL police training and criminal justice sector development for an additional $170 million. And of that, $160 million is being used to build seven police training centers for training 20,000 police by June, and $10 million is being used to develop the justice sector.

In short, we are seeking to prevent the institutionalization of the heroin cartels, to support democracy's early days in post-Taliban Afghanistan, to reinforce the best instincts of a people now freeing themselves from the terrorist's yoke, and to confront those that still threaten to destabilize that society through both narcotics trade and terrorism.

I will gladly add more detail later, but I will just say again, thank you for bringing this to the fore. And you have our pledge, my pledge, that we have a full court press on in both counter-narcotics and counterterrorism. Thank you.

Mr. SOUDER. Thank you very much for your testimony.

[The prepared statement of Mr. Charles follows:]

Testimony by
Robert B. Charles
Assistant Secretary of State
Bureau for
International Narcotics and Law Enforcement Affairs

House Committee on Government Reform
Subcommittee on Criminal Justice,
Drug Policy, and Human Resources

Thursday, February 26, 2004

Afghanistan: The Narcotics Situation and Strategy

Mr. Chairman, Committee members, I appreciate the opportunity to speak before you on the subject of "Afghanistan: The Narcotics Situation and Strategy."

The U.S. Government strategy for dealing with narcotics both within Afghanistan and trafficked from it is proactive and coordinated within the interagency. It is intended to reduce measurably heroin poppy cultivation, encourage alternative income streams, destroy drug labs, promote drug interdiction, and develop the justice sector to facilitate the proper prosecution and sentencing of traffickers. This State Department Bureau, the Bureau for International Narcotics and Law Enforcement Affairs (INL), is intent on working closely and effectively with both Congress and DEA to implement this strategy. In fact, the DEA Administrator and I have recently returned from a fact-finding trip to Afghanistan, where we represented the U.S. Government at the counter-drug conference in Kabul earlier this month.

Pieces of this counternarcotics strategy are proportionate to the urgency and needs presented on the ground. The various pieces of this emerging strategy are both complementary and independently important; the key words are proactive, comprehensive and accountable.

A few first impressions. My recent meeting with President Karzai reaffirmed my conviction that he means business – he is serious about tackling the heroin threat to his country. This is a leader who is dedicated to breaking the cycle of opium poppy cultivation and narcotics trafficking in his country before local trafficking rings become cartels and put down taproots, transforming Afghanistan into a narco-state. President Karzai is determined to proceed with every major aspect of breaking the heroin trade, even as he reinforces the productivity of alternative legitimate income streams, such as through the production of wheat, maize, barley and other needed crops.

As you know well, there are three essential components to our accelerating counter-narcotics strategy. The first component is targeted eradication of heroin poppies. The second is targeted, ever-widening availability and reinforcement of alternative streams of income. Democracies are consolidated not by reliance on drug money, but by pairing well-supported democratic institutions and the rule of law with a sound, growing, and free market in legitimate goods. Afghanistan has great needs, for example, in the area of legitimate agriculture. We intend to support the growth of a legitimate economy in that and other sectors.

Third, and finally, law enforcement, interdiction and justice sector reform are also key to success. We must raise the costs and risks of heroin trafficking, while raising the incentives for joining, or remaining part of, the legitimate economy. Only eight percent of Afghanistan's cultivated land is presently used to grow poppies, and we must make the incremental risk of its associated profits higher than the extra income it might produce.

There are other dangers from which we cannot avert our gaze. Afghanistan's heroin, which sells on the retail market for one hundred times the farm gate price, is the source of a growing reservoir of illegal money that funds international crime across the region, sustains the destabilizing activities of warlords, and fosters local coercion and terrorism. While available information about this pattern continues to grow, we cannot afford to stand by and wait as these destructive relationships and behaviors become clearer and institutionalized. Our comprehensive approach takes stock of these linkages, and is accelerating the effort to break each of them.

A few final thoughts. On eradication, some would argue – wait. Other priorities should trump this activity. I would argue swift action is essential. Distinguishing the urgent from the otherwise important requires that we tackle the poppy crop <u>now</u>.

Second, I can say without qualification that we have a committed ally in the Afghan government. President Karzai believes in democracy, the rule of law and human rights, and in a robust counter-narcotics effort. I see no signs of half-measures, and we are similarly committed.

Third, I am convinced that drug money and terrorist organizations in Afghanistan and throughout the region are locked together like chain links. While there may be other links in that chain, it is my conviction, based on the information available, that the two threats overlap palpably and incontrovertibly.

Fourth, we are cooperating closely with our European allies to support the Afghan government, particularly those with lead nation responsibilities. In that regard, we are pressing for increasing coordination with the British on counter-narcotics; with the Germans on policing; and with the Italians on justice sector reform.

Fifth, and finally, INL is determined to support and encourage cooperation between the efforts of the State Department, DEA, DoD, and USAID. Congress empowers us to achieve results for the American people, for the Afghan people and for greater local, regional and national security. Congress has funded the INL-coordinated portion of that effort with $50 million in supplemental appropriations in FY04, of which a significant portion will be dedicated to eradication.

Separately, Congress has funded INL police training and criminal justice sector development with an additional $120 million in 2004 supplemental funds, to which the Administration added $50 million in reprogrammed funds for accelerating success in Afghanistan, after appropriately notifying the Congress. Of this $170 million, $160 million is being used to build 7 police training centers to train at least 20,000 police by June, and $10 million is to develop the justice sector, including the training of judges and prosecutors, the building of courthouses, and the reinforcement of the rule of law through guidance on developing new laws, and the provision of technical assistance.

In short, we are seeking to prevent the institutionalization of heroin cartels, to support democracy's early days in post-Taliban Afghanistan, to reinforce the best instincts of a people now freeing themselves from the terrorists' yolk, and to confront those that still threaten to destabilize that society, through both the narcotics trade and terrorism.

This effort means being active in containing the narcotics trafficking threats in places like Turkmenistan, Uzbekistan, Tajikistan, the Kyrgyz Republic, Kazakhstan, and Pakistan, as well as points South and West. It means working with the United Nations office on Drugs and Crime (UNODC), strengthening our cooperation with DEA, focusing work with the G-8's June 2003 endorsement of the "Paris Pact" to zero-in on "drug routes" from Afghanistan to heroin markets, and demonstrating global leadership through our own efforts.

Mr. Chairman, INL is involved in a full-court press on both counter-narcotics and law enforcement in and around Afghanistan. These issues will not vanish overnight, but with congressional support and bipartisan cooperation in the knowledge that success in Afghanistan matters, we will, incrementally and collectively, succeed. Thank you.

Mr. SOUDER. And now I would like to move to Director Tandy.

STATEMENT OF KAREN P. TANDY, ADMINISTRATOR, DRUG ENFORCEMENT ADMINISTRATION

Ms. TANDY. Good afternoon, Chairman Souder, Ranking Member Cummings, and distinguished members of the committee. It is a privilege to appear before you today on behalf of the Drug Enforcement Administration to discuss our efforts to stem the flow of heroin from Afghanistan.

On behalf of the men and women of DEA, I particularly want to thank this subcommittee for your steadfast support for our efforts both on behalf of the agency and our mission.

Two weeks ago I returned from Afghanistan, and I saw for myself that the stakes in our war on narcotics there could scarcely be more urgent. Opium production has returned to nearly the same high levels as under the Taliban. This criminal trade feeds political and economic instability and provides fertile ground for the development of the sinister relationships to flourish between drug traffickers and terrorists. For those reasons, working in this region is a top priority for the Drug Enforcement Administration and for me.

I want to begin by describing our efforts, efforts undertaken in the face of a number of operational obstacles that we encounter daily in Afghanistan. Three decades of civil war and unrest have left the criminal justice system there without even its most basic elements. There is yet no developed police force, no prosecutors, no judges, and no prisons. The Afghan Counternarcotics Directorate is in its infancy, which leaves DEA with no viable national or local counterpart drug agency with which we can work.

Moreover, security constraints restrict our ability both to move within the country and to conduct our traditional drug investigations.

That said, DEA is a resourceful agency, and as such we are making considerable leeway—headway, rather—in the counternarcotics efforts in this region. We are seizing opportunities to disrupt Afghanistan's opium trade, deny terrorists a revenue source, and to inflict damage on the international drug markets. We are doing this principally in two ways. The first is interdiction. Like all other drug traffickers, Afghan trafficking organizations must move their illicit product to market. However, unlike most other source countries, Afghanistan is landlocked, and this forces the traffickers to rely on difficult and complex overland transshipment routes. DEA and our international counterparts are focused on various pressure points along these routes. Through Operation Containment, 19 countries, led by the Drug Enforcement Administration, are choking off the flow of drugs and precursor chemicals into and out of Afghanistan before they can spread to the broader markets. While Operation Containment has been under way for just 2 years, I am pleased to report that it is achieving great success. Since January 2003, Operation Containment has lead to 23 significant seizures of narcotics and precursor chemicals as well as the dismantlement and disruption of several major distribution and transportation organizations involved in the southwest Asian drug trade.

I would like to give you two quick examples of these successes. Most notably, Operation Containment has led to the disruption in

Istanbul of one of the most significant heroin trafficking organizations in Turkey, and resulted in an all-time record seizure of 7.4 tons of morphine base. I would like to note that this single 7.4 tons of morphine base, this single seizure is 4 times greater than the worldwide seizures in the year 2000 prior to Operation Containment.

The operation has also resulted in the seizure of over 1,000 kilograms of heroin in Turkey and the arrest of several traffickers. It is reported to be, as I said, the largest heroin seizure in Turkey's history.

Operation Containment also has built law enforcement cooperation throughout the region. And as a result of these growing partnerships, a joint investigation by the Drug Enforcement Administration and our Turkish and Russian counterparts resulted in the seizure in Turkey of 4 tons of acetic anhydride, which is the chemical used in the production of heroin.

In addition, the seizure of 17 tons of acetic anhydride at a border crossing in Turkey led to an additional 5.5 tons of the chemical buried at a Turkish farm.

The second way we are attacking the Afghan opium trade is by working in country with our coalition partners. I have directed DEA's agents in our Kabul, Afghanistan office to aggressively focus their intelligence collection on identifying heroin processing labs, and sharing that information with the Afghan authorities and our allies among the coalition partners.

DEA strongly supports the Defense Department's initiative to open an intelligence fusion center in Afghanistan in order to multinationally share information.

In addition, our offices in Kabul and throughout the region are focused on identifying the major trafficking organizations and their money flow so that we can strategically attack them where they are most vulnerable, whether inside Afghanistan or elsewhere in the region.

After my recent visit to Kabul and my discussions with the U.S. Ambassador there, I am particularly pleased to report that DEA will be and is now working to significantly expand our presence in Afghanistan and in Kabul.

As this subcommittee knows, the challenges to the counternarcotics efforts in Afghanistan and the region are great, but the stabilization—excuse me, the opportunities to take down the drug trade and support stabilization are just as great. And for this reason I am cautiously optimistic about the future of our drug enforcement efforts in Afghanistan.

In my written testimony I've addressed DEA's initiatives in the region in greater detail, and I would be delighted to answer any questions the committee may have. Thank you.

[The prepared statement of Ms. Tandy follows:]

Statement of

Karen P. Tandy
Administrator

Drug Enforcement Administration

Before the

Subcommittee on Criminal Justice, Drug Policy and Human Resources
Committee on Government Reform
U.S. House of Representatives

February 26, 2004

"Afghanistan: Law Enforcement Interdiction Efforts in Transshipment Countries to Stem the Flow of Heroin"

Chairman Souder, Ranking Member Cummings and distinguished members of the Subcommittee, thank you for the invitation to testify today on the important issue of disrupting the market for Afghan heroin.

Overview

Afghan drug production is a priority for the DEA that guides our enforcement strategy in the region. As you know, opium production in Afghanistan has resumed over the last two years, although it is still lower than the highest level reached under the Taliban. While we expect that only a small portion of the resulting opium and heroin will ultimately reach the United States, these drugs are of great concern because they increase worldwide supply and have the potential to fund terrorists and other destabilizing groups. Because the situation inside Afghanistan presents unique challenges to law enforcement, the DEA has successfully acted to control the spread of Afghan opium and heroin in the surrounding nations through Operation Containment.

Two weeks ago, I returned from Kabul where Assistant Secretary of State Robert Charles, other senior officials representing the United States, and I participated in discussions with Afghanistan Transitional Authority President Hamid Karzai, United Nations Office of Drugs and Crime Director Antonio Costa and other representatives from Afghanistan and the European Union on the challenges posed by Afghan drug production. As a result of my visit and discussions with Ambassador Khalilzad, the DEA intends to significantly expand its presence in Afghanistan as well as intelligence collection connected to our broader efforts to control transshipment through the region. I look forward to discussing each of these important issues with the Subcommittee.

Afghanistan Poppy Production and the U.S. Response

Significant Opium Production Resumes

Afghanistan is a major source country for the cultivation, processing and trafficking of opiate products. It has historically produced significant quantities of opium, and accounted for over 70 percent of the world's supply in the year 2000, when the United States government estimated Afghan opium production at 3,656 metric tons. In 2001, the Taliban banned the cultivation of opium poppy. The DEA believes that the ban was likely an attempt by the Taliban to raise the price of opium which had fallen significantly due to the abundant supply produced in years prior to 2001. Regardless of intent, production plummeted to 74 metric tons in 2001.

With the fall of the Taliban, Afghan growers resumed cultivation despite renewal of the ban on poppy growth by the Karzai government. Opium production has returned to its historically substantial amounts, although it is important to emphasize that it has not yet reached the level of poppy recorded in 2000. In 2003, the United States Government officially estimated production of 2,865 metric tons of oven-dried opium from 61,000 hectares of poppy cultivation.

Afghanistan: Estimated Annual Potential Opium Production (Metric Tons)

2003	2002	2001	2000	1999	1998	1997	1996
2,865	1,278	74	3,656	2,861	2,340	2,184	2,099

Heroin Production and Movement

The opium produced in Afghanistan is readily made into narcotics to be sold on the international market, much of which eventually reaches users in Europe. While Europe is the primary destination for Afghan heroin, much of the opium remains in Southwest Asia for local consumption. Laboratories convert the opium into morphine base, white heroin, or one of several grades of brown heroin. Large processing laboratories are primarily located in southern Afghanistan; smaller laboratories are located in other areas of the country, including the Nangarhar Province. In addition, morphine base produced in Afghanistan is shipped to traffickers based in Turkey and converted to heroin.

Transporting converted opium from Afghanistan is no easy task. Larger than the State of Texas, Afghanistan is landlocked, forcing traffickers to rely on challenging overland routes to move drug shipments out of the country. In addition to the traditional smuggling routes through Iran to Turkey, our intelligence reports indicate continued movement of heroin shipments north from Afghanistan through the Central Asian States, notably Tajikistan, to Russia. Some of the heroin is consumed in Russia, while a portion moves on to other markets. Afghan heroin also moves through India enroute to international markets and continues to be trafficked through Pakistan, where heroin is smuggled out through airports and vessels leaving the Pakistan coast.

DEA intelligence suggests that relatively little Afghan heroin is ultimately destined for the United States, although we continue to monitor carefully the market for potential new trends. Through the Heroin Signature Program (HSP), the DEA Special Testing and Research Laboratory analyzes samples from seizures at ports of entry and other randomly selected sources to determine their purity and geographic origin. In 2002, Southwest Asian heroin (which includes Afghan heroin) accounted for ten percent of the weight of all samples analyzed. Preliminary data for 2003 indicate that Southwest Asian heroin was eight percent by weight of the sample, although the 2003 survey is not yet complete. Similarly, the Domestic Monitor Program (DMP), which examines samples bought undercover on American streets to monitor their characteristics, showed that Southwest Asian heroin represented four percent of samples in 2002 and five percent in 2003. Neither HSP nor DMP results should be equated with market share, but rather suggest availability over time.

It is important to remember, however, that the past can be a prologue. In 1984, as much as 50% of the heroin in the American market originated in the Afghanistan/Pakistan border area. We must appreciate history and diligently work to foreclose the return of Afghan heroin to the American market.

The DEA's Response Inside Afghanistan

Opium production in Afghanistan is a significant concern and a priority for the DEA because of its impact on worldwide drug supply and its potential, as I will discuss later, to provide financial support to terrorists and other destabilizing groups. In assessing strategies to control and respond to this production, it is important to understand the significant operational obstacles we face in Afghanistan. Three decades of civil war and unrest have left the criminal justice system in disarray. Outside of Kabul, the country is not uniformly controlled by the central government. The Afghan Counter Narcotics Directorate is in its infancy stage of development, leaving the DEA with no viable national or local drug enforcement counterparts. Afghanistan also lacks many of the most basic elements of its criminal justice institutions.

Due to security constraints, the DEA's presence in Afghanistan has been limited to two agents, whose movement and ability to conduct traditional drug enforcement operations have been severely restricted. Our Kabul Country Office, reopened in February 2003, nonetheless has made superb contributions under these difficult circumstances. DEA agents have continued to gather and disseminate intelligence to U.S. and British law enforcement and intelligence agencies. Because the collection and analysis of drug intelligence within Afghanistan and Central Asia feeds our overall enforcement efforts in the region, we have made it a priority and are also supporting a Department of Defense initiative to open an intelligence "fusion center" in Afghanistan for multinational information sharing. Our country office also continues to collect significant amounts of human intelligence from our confidential sources in Kabul and supports domestic and foreign drug enforcement operations.

After my recent visit to Kabul and discussions with Ambassador Khalilzad, I am pleased to let you know that the DEA will be working to significantly expand its presence in Kabul from existing resources of our Office of International Operations. I have also directed my agents to aggressively focus on identifying heroin processing labs and sharing that information with the Afghan authorities and our coalition partners. Our offices in Kabul and throughout the region will place particular emphasis on working with our partners to identify the major trafficking organizations and their money flow so we can strategically attack them where they are most vulnerable, whether inside Afghanistan or in the region.

The DEA's Regional Initiatives

Operation Containment

The challenges to law enforcement within Afghanistan strongly suggested the need for a simultaneous, concerted effort to control Afghan drugs in neighboring countries before they can spread to broader markets. Operation Containment is a large-scale, multinational law enforcement initiative begun in early 2002 under the leadership of the DEA and with special support from Congress. Emphasizing coordination and information sharing among nineteen countries from Central Asia, the Caucuses, Europe and Russia, the program aims to implement a joint strategy to deprive drug trafficking organizations of their market access and international terrorist groups of financial support from drugs, precursor chemicals, weapons, ammunition and currency. It has been enormously successful, and I would like to thank the Subcommittee for its strong support for this initiative and the opportunity to highlight it today.

The DEA supports Operation Containment worldwide, particularly in Pakistan, Turkey, Russia, and Central Asia. We have expanded existing offices in Europe and Southwest Asia and opened a new office in Uzbekistan. The DEA has assigned Special Agents to its Kabul, Ankara, Istanbul, Tashkent, Moscow and London Offices to support Operation Containment. In addition, one Intelligence Specialist and one support position are assigned in Ankara and one support position is assigned in Tashkent to support Operation Containment. DEA is also seeking approval to assign two Special Agents to Kyrgyzstan and additional agent and intelligence personnel to Uzbekistan and Belgium for Operation Containment.

Another key element is the Sensitive Investigative Unit (SIU), a program that has been highly successful in other regions of the world. An SIU is made up of host nation law enforcement personnel, who are individually screened to protect against corruption and then specially trained and equipped to DEA standards. We have established a new DEA SIU in Uzbekistan, and the DEA SIU in Pakistan has made several significant seizures. These DEA-lead units provide critical and valuable assistance to anti-drug efforts in their countries.

Intelligence sharing is also a priority of Operation Containment, with the initiative supporting regional intelligence sharing centers in Bucharest, Romania and Bishkek,

Kyrgyzstan and a short-term Fusion Center program in Tashkent, Uzbekistan. DEA has temporarily assigned an Intelligence Analyst to the Bucharest intelligence center.

Operation Containment has been a great success. Since March 2002, it has resulted in 23 significant seizures of narcotics and precursor chemicals and led to the dismantlement and disruption of several major distribution/transportation organizations involved in the Southwest Asian drug trade. These include the disruption three months ago in Istanbul of the Galip Kuyucu transportation group, which was one of the most significant heroin traffickers in Turkey and a Justice Department international priority target. The Turkish National Police, working with the DEA and Her Majesty's Customs and Excise, seized 495 kilograms of heroin, and disrupted this organization, which was regularly transporting similarly sized amounts of drugs throughout Western Europe. This investigation also led to the arrest of Urfi Cetinkaya, a major source of heroin supply with direct ties to Afghan drug traffickers.

Another significant success for Operation Containment was the arrest of 15 members of the Attila Ozyildirim heroin trafficking organization and the seizure of 7.4 tons of morphine base in Turkey during March 2002. This is the largest seizure of morphine base ever made. To put the magnitude of this seizure in perspective - the amount seized was more than four times greater than the total worldwide morphine base seizures made in 2000. Morphine base can be converted to heroin at a ratio of 1:1.

Drug Enforcement Training

The DEA is also working to build law enforcement capability and cooperation in Afghanistan and throughout the region. During October 2002, we participated along with officials from Afghanistan's Interior Ministry in a United Nations International Narcotics Control Board conference in Tashkent, Uzbekistan regarding Operation Topaz. Operation Topaz is intended to bring together law enforcement in several nations to detect and seize suspicious and unauthorized shipments of acetic anhydride, the primary precursor chemical used in the production of heroin.

This initiative and other enforcement efforts have led to several significant seizures in Turkey, Russia, Bosnia Herzegovina, Serbia, Bulgaria, and other countries. Two examples particularly demonstrate the mutual benefit of our partnerships and joint efforts. A joint investigation by the DEA, the Turkish National Police, and the Russian MV resulted in the seizure of four tons of acetic anhydride in Turkey during December 2002, which in turn led to seizure of an additional 3,200 kilograms of acetic anhydride in Bryansk, Russia in April 2003. Similarly, the seizure in August 2002 of 17 tons of acetic anhydride at a border crossing in Ipsala, Turkey that had originated in Macedonia led to an additional 5.5 tons of the chemical buried in a Turkish farm.

We have also particularly emphasized training for foreign law enforcement agencies, including a three week seminar conducted last September in the United States for high-level police managers. General Hilaluddin Hilal, Afghanistan's Deputy Interior Minister of Security Affairs, attended the course, which took place at both DEA

Headquarters and the DEA Academy in Quantico, Virginia. I participated in this seminar personally as did members of the DEA's senior management, and we believe that it helped to begin and improve important partnerships with and among DEA and the international agencies involved.

During 2004, the DEA plans to conduct Drug Unit Commander training courses in Turkey and Uzbekistan. These one-week courses are funded through Operation Containment and are geared for supervisors of operational drug units. We anticipate that five to ten participants from throughout Afghanistan will attend each school. In addition, DEA is expanding its training efforts throughout the region during 2004, with training courses scheduled in Turkmenistan, Uzbekistan, Tajikistan, Thailand and India.

Links between Terrorism and the Afghan Drug Trade

Mr. Chairman, I would also like to briefly discuss the potential links between terrorism and trafficking of Afghan opium and heroin, which provide an important rationale for our efforts in the region. Last September, President Bush thanked DEA agents in a speech at Quantico, Virginia. He said "By keeping drug money from financing terror, you're playing an important part of this war." And we will continue doing so not only through drug investigations potentially tied to terrorists and those who fund them, but also through the DEA's renewed emphasis on financial investigations intended to deprive all drug traffickers of their evil profits.

Raw intelligence and uncorroborated confidential sources continue to indicate possible relationships between drug traffic and terrorist groups within Afghanistan. The DEA will continue to assign the highest priority to investigating any information linking drugs to terrorism. We will do so in cooperation with our law enforcement and intelligence partners, and we will aggressively work to gather and document intelligence relating to drug activity that may finance terrorism.

My broader efforts as Administrator to renew the DEA's emphasis on financial investigations will also enhance our ability to reach potential terrorist funding. In addition to creating a new DEA Office of Financial Operations and money laundering groups in each field division, I have directed that illegal drug proceeds financing terrorism should be of the highest priority for those investigations. The Drug/Financial Fusion Center recently created by Congress will also use the Foreign Terrorist Tracking Task Force's architecture to enhance capabilities to uncover links between drug trafficking and terrorism. Investigative links between drug trafficking and money laundering organizations and known terrorist organizations will be shared with the FBI, the Department of Homeland Security, the Treasury Department and the intelligence community. Our intelligence programs continue to work closely with law enforcement and the intelligence community to identify and anticipate emerging threats posed by the links between drug trafficking and terrorism.

Conclusion

Mr. Chairman, control of drugs produced in Afghanistan both within the country and throughout the region is an agencywide priority for the DEA. I very much appreciate the opportunity to testify before the Subcommittee today. I will be happy to answer any questions you may have.

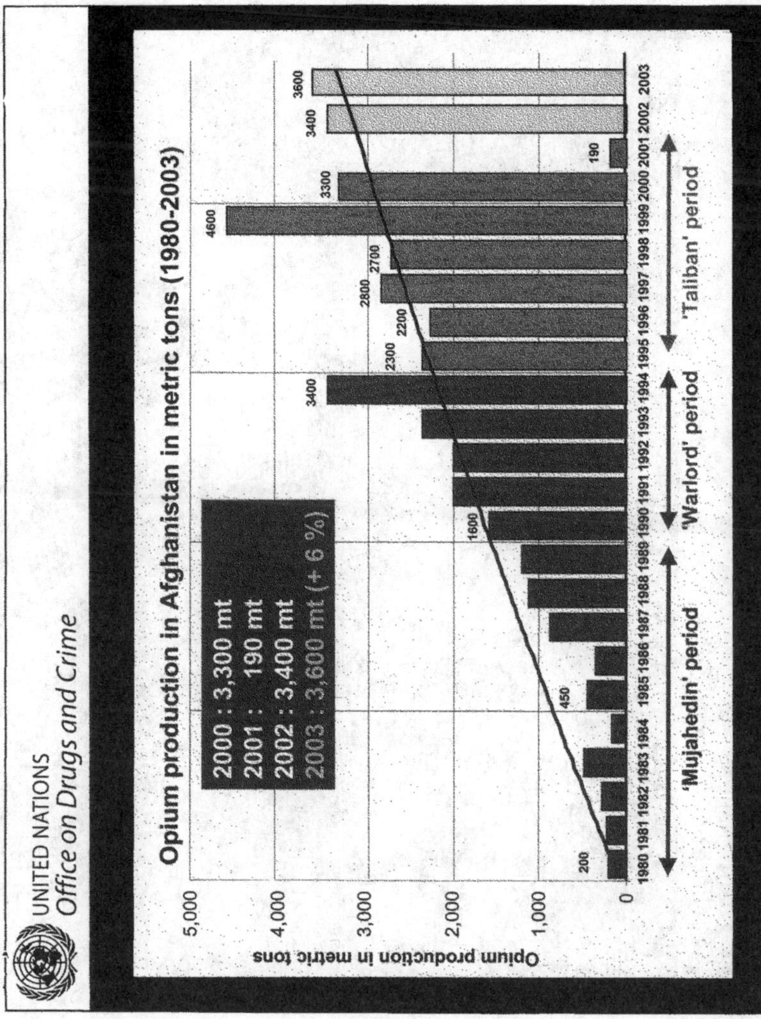
UNITED NATIONS
Office on Drugs and Crime
Opium production in Afghanistan in metric tons (1980-2003)
2000 : 3,300 mt
2001 : 190 mt
2002 : 3,400 mt
2003 : 3,600 mt (+ 6 %)
Opium production in metric tons
0
1,000
2,000
3,000
4,000
5,000
200
450
1600
3400
2300
2200
2800
2700
4600
3300
190
3400
3600
1980 1981 1982 1983 1984 1985 1986 1987 1988 1989 1990 1991 1992 1993 1994 1995 1996 1997 1998 1999 2000 2001 2002 2003
'Mujahedin' period
'Warlord' period
'Taliban' period

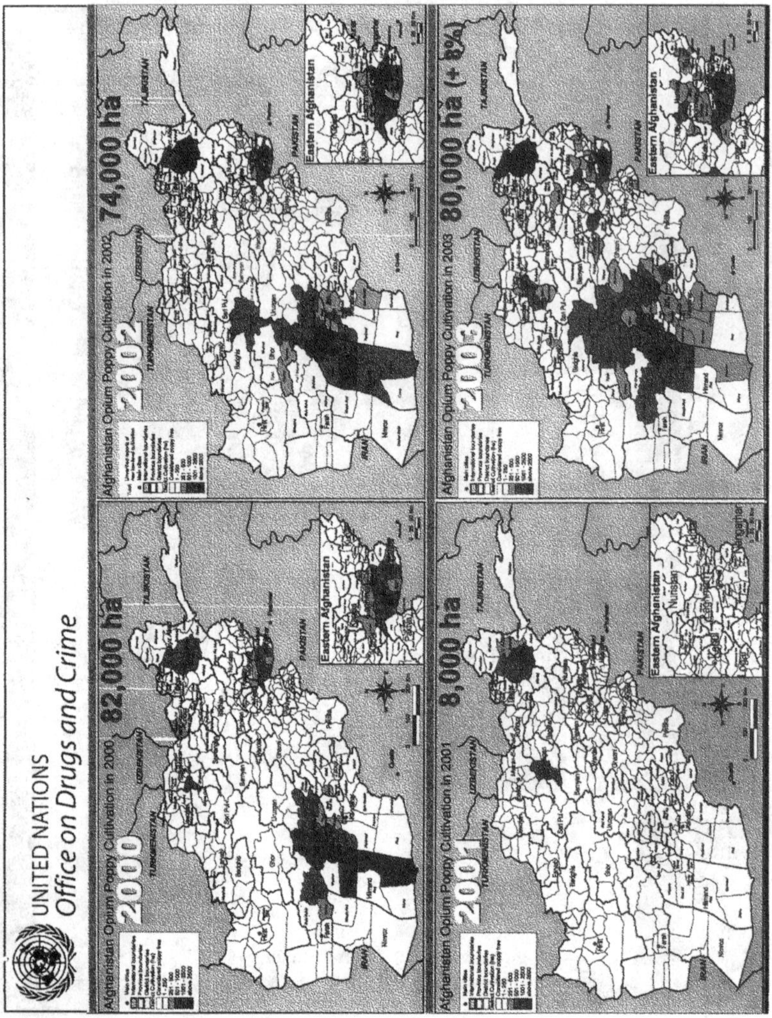
UNITED NATIONS
Office on Drugs and Crime
Afghanistan Opium Poppy Cultivation in 2000
2000
82,000 ha
Afghanistan Opium Poppy Cultivation in 2002
2002
74,000 ha
Afghanistan Opium Poppy Cultivation in 2001
2001
8,000 ha
Afghanistan Opium Poppy Cultivation in 2003
2003
80,000 ha (+ 8%)
Eastern Afghanistan

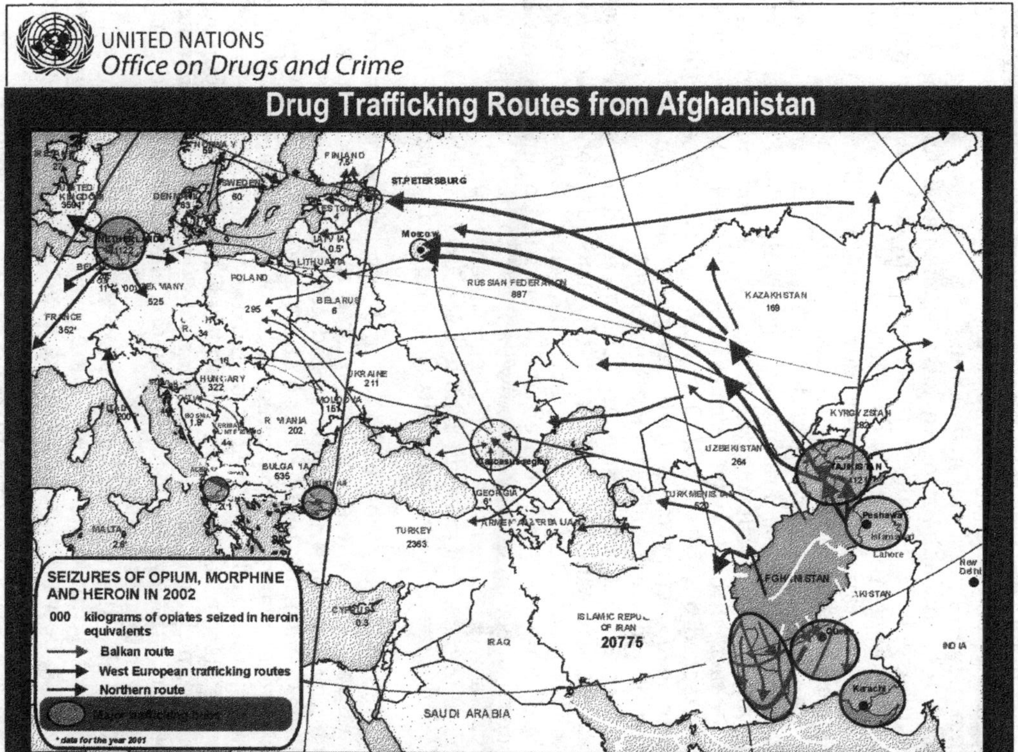
UNITED NATIONS
Office on Drugs and Crime
Drug Trafficking Routes from Afghanistan
FINLAND 7.5*
ST.PETERSBURG
SWEDEN 60
Moscow
LATVIA 0.5*
LITHUANIA
POLAND
GERMANY 525
FRANCE 352*
BELARUS 6
RUSSIAN FEDERATION 887
KAZAKHSTAN 169
UKRAINE 211
HUNGARY 322
ROMANIA 202
BULGARIA 535
MOLDOVA 151
MALTA 2.8
GEORGIA 6*
TURKEY 2363
UZBEKISTAN 264
KYRGYZSTAN
TAJIKISTAN
AFGHANISTAN
PAKISTAN
Peshawar
Lahore
New Delhi
INDIA
Karachi
CYPRUS 0.3
IRAQ
ISLAMIC REPUBLIC OF IRAN 20775
SAUDI ARABIA
SEIZURES OF OPIUM, MORPHINE AND HEROIN IN 2002
000 kilograms of opiates seized in heroin equivalents
Balkan route
West European trafficking routes
Northern route
Major trafficking hubs
* data for the year 2001

Mr. SOUDER. We have also been joined by Congressman Carter. I appreciate his being with us as well.

I am going to start the questioning. I assume we will go several rounds. It's unusual for us to have a one-panel hearing, but we want to explore this subject relatively thoroughly. We have been having meetings the last few days as well.

But let me start with my first round with Mr. Charles, that British government officials had told me a little over a year ago and have told our staff more recently that attacking strategic targets like opium warehouses and processing plants would have an enormous impact on disrupting the trade in and around Afghanistan. And, in fact, in one of the articles in the Financial Times it says they attacked one in early January. Why have these facilities not already been destroyed? And what is the explanation for lack of action on this matter? And who is responsible?

It appears from your testimony that we're all of a sudden becoming aggressive, which is really laudable. The question is, how do we get to this point? And are those barriers being lifted? Did you sense the barriers were there before? Could you kind of discuss this fundamental question of why, since we appear to have had quite a bit of this knowledge, actions hadn't been taken up until now?

Mr. CHARLES. Let me say I have been on this job for 120 days, so I will take full responsibility for everything during that 120 days.

But let me also go beyond that and say the point you make is a good one, that there are many force multipliers in a world in which you have not institutionalized the heroin market yet. And what do I mean by that? I mean there are no heroin cartels. You have several warlords who make a lot of money on this. And you are absolutely right, that if you can target the places that they keep the heroin, the labs in which they create the heroin out of heroin poppies, you can disrupt that market in ways that probably go beyond what we could do anywhere else in the world because it is not yet institutionalized.

Let me say also that while there are many force multipliers, this is one that I think the entire interagency process is beginning to realize can be very significant. And as you indicated, there was at least one recent example where this occurred.

From the State Department point of view, we are working hard to spur greater intelligence sharing, greater information sharing across all the spectrums, so that when you come up with CN intelligence, counternarcotics intelligence, it's shared broadly; if you come up with counterterrorism intelligence and it happens to bump into things that relate to narcotics, that is shared broadly.

We are also, obviously, moving out into the field ourselves to try to kill the poppies, and obviously that will have a force multiplier effect.

The specific question about could more be done: And I can't speak to the question of whether more could have been done in the past, but I can speak to the question as to whether or not more will be done in the future. And I think we have a stronger and stronger working relationship with the Department of Defense. My understanding is that there is some guidance, I haven't seen it yet, that would indicate that when the Department of Defense finds, in the course of a counterterrorism mission, narcotics, they are able to then either destroy it directly—I think that's what they will do—or be able to empower others to do that.

We are also supporting the British. And you mentioned the British. They are active in the field, and we are supporting them in a number of ways. And I have been pressing them as the assistant secretary to do more, and I am actually encouraging them that we think we can do more with them.

So the short answer is I think you are going to see maybe not an exponential change but a marked increase in interagency coordination and probably the international or multinational coordination on this. And that is critical as a force multiplier.

Mr. SOUDER. Without getting into, because I don't have all the information, so I'm not attempting to get into classified materials. But we are all pretty aware that there is another agency involved as well that's on the ground with contract employees. Is the CIA a part of these interagency teams? And how is that working as you move into the different zones?

Mr. CHARLES. Well, let me address it in an unclassified way and put the chart on the wall, so people can see it, something I asked to be declassified.

There is a chart which is up on the wall now which you will see indicates, in an unclassified or declassified way, that there are four terrorist organizations that we know are involved in Afghanistan: Hezbe-Islami, HIG, Taliban, Islamic Movement of Uzbekistan, and al Qaeda. At varying degrees of connectivity or connectedness, you can see that these organizations have some relationship, we think, to the drug trade. And you can see again, based on the color coding, that some of them are stronger, almost definitely involved in one way or another, and others are possibly involved.

What I would say to you is that my sense, from where I sit, is that there is an increasing degree of interagency coordination on information sharing, and that the greatest force multiplier of all is the sharing of information. At the end of the day, we have to have people in the country that can do this job, we have to be all of us commited to the same mission. And I would also add that we do not want, and I certainly would never advocate, that we diminish in any way the counterterrorism effort just because we are also driving hard to eliminate the counternarcotics, the narcotics problem.

But I would end it by saying—my answer—by saying the reason I think that everybody working together on the counternarcotics piece is so important is that you cannot erect a lasting castle on sand and you cannot erect a lasting democracy on a heroin economy.

Mr. SOUDER. We haven't necessarily made government more efficient, but we have had some clarification of roles, at least in a theoretical way, with the organization of the Department of Homeland Security, with the FBI taking a more security orientation, with the military having a more military mission, and the CIA having multitasking but more on terrorism and security risks of the United States. Which has left, at least theoretically, DEA as the primary narcotics agency, and has the money in your area inside State as the primary narcotics area. That isn't saying Homeland

Security doesn't have large chunks, too, and the old Border Patrol and Customs. But your relationship between the two of you becomes more critical.

You announced a number of new initiatives that you are undertaking. Have you talked those through with the DEA and you are going to coordinate those, in particular, with them?

Mr. CHARLES. Well, I will let Karen speak to that issue in terms of the many discussions and the support that we provide and her view of the support that we provide.

Let me say that my view is that we are working very closely together on a number of fronts. There are things called sensitive investigative units that since about 2000 we have begun to work even more closely on. We are highly supportive of DEA, not only in Afghanistan, but, as you have indicated and as other members have indicated, in surrounding countries because containment is terribly important.

Containment always reminds me of the cold war era word "containment." And I am reminded of what Ronald Reagan did shortly thereafter, which is to move to what he called "rollback," which is to move even further and more aggressively.

And if I were to characterize where we are going, I would say I hope that the place we are going is to roll back the whole trafficker environment so that we can stabilize all of these countries more directly. But I think we have a close working relationship that is, in fact, leading in this area.

Mr. SOUDER. Thank you.

Mr. Cummings.

Mr. CUMMINGS. Mr. Charles, the UNODC's 2003 estimate suggested the Afghan opium output reached record levels last year and accounted for about 75 percent of the opium production worldwide. What explains that explosive figure?

Mr. CHARLES. Let me take a short stab at that and say, incidentally, I think it was the second highest year rather than the highest year. But that is not to say that it isn't a matter of enormous concern.

You have a country in which survival tends to be the driving force right now. Farmers, as I indicated in my testimony, make about a dollar for the same quantity of heroin that shows up on the streets of Paris and commands a price of $100, or the streets of New York, by the way, or the streets of Baltimore where you have been a leader, and this is a genuine problem.

What has transpired, I think, is that as the government, the central government has gotten more in control of the environment, as the interagency process—and we have migrated from a military mission which was dedicated to counterterrorism into an environment where we see both counterterrorism and counternarcotics as mutually or equally important, or both of them very important for the long term. We have migrated the whole strategy. There has been a ponying up of dollars. The dollars this year, we have $170 million to work with on policing. And we do all the policing, by the way, at INL, too. We have seven police academies that we are getting off the ground in Afghanistan. But there has also been a supplemental of $50 million, which allows us for the first time to aggressively go and eradicate.

And I want to illustrate—and I'm not sure we can put this up on the wall, but there is a picture. This chart illustrates how the—on the right-hand side as you look at it—how these plots are largely done. It takes manual eradication or an incentivizing structure to get people out of the business of growing them. Because you cannot do aerial eradication in Afghanistan the way you can on Colombia.

In Colombia we are making some significant progress with the Colombian Government on aerial eradication. Here, it's going to be manual and it's going to be driven by incentives and it's going to be driven by a number of factors which, frankly, have only just begun to coalesce. And so I would tell you that as with any major undertaking, including, incidentally, Plan Colombia, it takes a couple of years to get the process in motion. And what happened is there was a gap in time between when the Taliban were thrown out of government and the military was stabilizing the country. And you could actually initiate under the leadership of President Karzai a program that would actively work on both eradication and a number of other components.

Remember, too—I guess I would just say that it's hard to imagine what we are confronting in Afghanistan. The way I would describe it is that it's as if someone said to you, you have to build a house tomorrow, within 24 hours, and you have to pour the foundation and put the roof on and stud up the walls and put windows in and put doors in all at once. And my pledge to you is we are trying to do that. But the eradication piece is coming on line now because, literally, it took time to put these pieces in place. And you, Congress, have given us the money to do this, and I am grateful for that and we are driving ahead full force to do that.

Mr. CUMMINGS. Ms. Tandy, you know, I think it was the last Super Bowl, I saw these commercials where they were saying—talking about the relationship between terrorist organizations and the drugs on our streets. And, you know, I was just trying to figure out, where do you see, how does the—how would you rank the Afghan drug trade in terms of threats to our security in this country?

And then I want you to comment, maybe both of you, but Ms. Tandy you talked about no judges, no prosecution, no prisons. You know, it just seems like it's almost an impossible task. I mean, we talk about a thin blue line in the United States with regard to policing. But, there, there is no line. And I know you just talked about your seven training facilities and—but what, how do you deal with that? I mean, you catch somebody, and is that do they—I mean, what do you do?

Ms. TANDY. Taking it in the order that you asked, Representative Cummings, the Afghan heroin threat to this country can be measured in terms of raw numbers, that which is heroin that makes it into this country from Afghanistan and in that region. We are still compiling the actual numbers from our two programs that help us measure that: the heroin signature program, which measures the samples of heroin coming into the country at ports of entry to determine what the source is, what country source or what regional source the heroin is arriving to the United States from; and our domestic monitoring program where we buy samples of heroin and have that tested, again, to determine the regional source.

For us, 20 years ago in this country, Afghanistan represented 50 percent of the supply of heroin to the United States. It is and has been around 7 to 10 percent. We won't know the final numbers for this past year until sometime in September when all of those samples have been analyzed. But that is a clear threat to our country, including Baltimore and this northeast corridor in particular, where heroin is especially problematic for us.

In terms of the——

Mr. CUMMINGS. Where does the rest of it go?

Ms. TANDY. I'm sorry?

Mr. CUMMINGS. Where does the rest of it go? You accounted for 7 percent. Where does the 93 percent go? Europe?

Ms. TANDY. A great portion of that goes to Europe, certainly the UK, which is why they have the lead on counternarcotics in Afghanistan among the coalition partners.

Mr. CUMMINGS. And when you say they have the lead, it seems like quite often when the United States is involved we seem to—we may, even if we are not leading, although we usually are, it seems like we are putting in a whole lot of resources, and sometimes others who benefit greatly are not putting in as much. Now, does the lead also go to how much money they are putting in?

Mr. CHARLES. Let me address that, if I may, because that is something that I ask about regularly. In both my former life and in this life, it's certainly worried me that we are proportionately carrying a lot of the burden; historically have. But let me say, both in addressing your question, your earlier question, but also on the dollar question, actually for this hearing I broke it out, and we have about $130 million in counternarcotics programs that the British are pressing forward over a 3-year period. We have an additional commitment of 2 million and change to press this immediate initiative on eradication. They will also—and there is some components you may want to be briefed on, that can't be discussed in this hearing, that the British are actively involved in, that I think are highly supportive of the interdiction effort on balance. We have asked them to pony up, and they have done so in a number of other areas that involve information sharing.

I have another list I will give you of other countries. Don't—please don't take away from what I'm saying that I am satisfied that we are proportionately—I believe that they are the lead and they are doing a lot, but I think all of us and I think collectively can do more. And that is one of the things I am personally pushing for.

I want to address four points that really come to your—the four questions, sort of subsidiary questions that I think you just asked.

One is the impact on this country in heroin. And I want to tell you that every piece of information I have supports what the administrator just said, which is that 7 to 10 percent of the heroin on our streets today is Afghan or at least southeast Asian—and southwest Asian heroin. The significance of that—people say that's not enough for us to care a whole lot about that problem versus, let's say, the Colombian heroin which shows up, up and down the eastern corridor. I tell you that my view is that we have about a million addicts in this country, heroin addicts. That's 70,000 to

100,000 souls right there. So that's enough reason for me to be involved.

The second thing I would say on the terrorism threat. You will notice that in the chart that I provided, you have al Qaeda and a number of other groups that are involved. Historically, and to this day, we do not have what I would call evidence of—in a case-making way on individuals beyond those that have already been apprehended, but we do have something that is almost as strong for warfighting purposes and for protecting our national security, and that is very strong indications, objective indications that there is a very tight overlap between heroin—drugs, Afghan drugs, heroin, and the terrorist organizations that are there. And what that means is that if you took two circles and drew them on a sheet of paper, and one was drug traffickers and one was known terrorist organizations, they would overlap each other, in my view, on the information that I know, substantially.

So that's the second piece. National security is protected by being aggressive in knocking out the funding source for terrorism, and Afghan heroin is a part of that.

The third thing is the justice sector. You are right, it is—as I indicated in terms of the building of a house, it is a very difficult thing to do everything at once, but—so that there isn't a sense of utter hopelessness, and in fact I would urge hopefulness—what we are able to do is a targeted process of apprehending drug traffickers. What I foresee happening is we will apprehend, with the Afghan Government, drug traffickers. There are prisons, there aren't a lot of them. There will be courthouses. We are putting $10 million in right now to the building or rebuilding of courthouses. We are training judges. The INL is doing this. We are training prosecutors. There will be, in fairly short order, the ability in a targeted way to send a message that drug trafficking and criminal activity of this kind is not tolerated in a free and democratic and noncorrupt Afghanistan. And that's part of what we are doing.

The final question you asked was with respect to police. And I would tell you again that we are at the beginning of a process that I find far more hopeful than I often read in the media. I think we have a great deal of reason to be hopeful about the future. We are on track. And I say to you, every barometer—and I check this every day, and we had a big meeting yesterday and I talked with the Ambassador. We are on track to produce 20,000 police, at least, by June. And in that process, in the seven academies which will bear, each one of them, about—they will have a capacity for about 1,250 each. We have the instructors. We are moving it forward. There is no problem with the recruits that we know of.

We are moving forward, with the leadership of the Afghan government, to generate a secure environment. And I think—all I would tell you is keep bringing us back in front of you. Keep asking us these questions and asking us if we are making progress. And to date, because I am very much an honest broker and feel that in many ways I am an oversight guy who happens to be working in program administration, that we are on track. And to that end I give you, I guess, a little more encouraging message.

Ms. TANDY. Representative Cummings, if I could just add with regard to your question about the justice sector obstacles for us. It is precisely the lack of institutions currently in Afghanistan that makes Operation Containment so critical. With the seizures, prosecution of those who are trafficking the heroin through the region into Europe and elsewhere, that is where we are able to have the greatest enforcement impact currently, until these institutions do mature, do stand up in Afghanistan.

I also have met with our British counterparts and discussed with them our statutory framework under 21 U.S.C. 959, which has an extraterritorial jurisdiction provision and has been applied most effectively against Colombian traffickers, where those who never leave Colombia but are sending drugs into the United States from Colombia are charged in the United States and extradited from Colombia or expelled for prosecution in the United States simply because they knew or intended to send drugs to the United States. We are trying to apply that same statutory framework to Afghanistan, to remove those trafficking organizations in Afghanistan and prosecute them in the United States, to the extent that we can, through intelligence and our enforcement efforts, make those linkages as to intent; and, if not to the United States, to the U.K. Under this same kind of statutory framework. And we are working with them to develop that procedure in the U.K.

Mr. CUMMINGS. Thank you very much.

Mr. SOUDER. Congressman Carter.

Mr. CARTER. Thank you, Mr. Chairman.

I have just returned from Afghanistan. I was there last week. We had an opportunity to meet with President Karzai, with the Ambassador, our Ambassador, and with folks within their Defense Department and their State Department. And when it was my turn to ask the question, this was my question: Let's talk about the drug situation here in Afghanistan, and what are you going to do about it? He gave very positive, very direct answers that it's a major concern. He's on board. He mentioned the DEA was doing outstanding work there.

But the underlying theme to me—and I'm not speaking negatively; I was very positively impressed by the President and his cabinet. But I was—I felt an underlying theme that they've got a whole lot more problems than this right now, and this is their cash crop. And it really is. And they don't have political parties and they are about to try to hold elections this summer, a whole lot of the police force is going to be tied up trying to keep things in control. That's the most heavily armed bunch of civilians on the face of the Earth. And I asked the general how he distinguished a bad guy from a good guy, and he said: A good guy only has two clips of ammunition; a bad guy either has hand grenades or more than two clips of ammunition. It's a very difficult problem in Afghanistan to deal with.

And I think they overall are on board to try to do something with this, but it's a farmer problem. And to me, and I asked this question, it's a processor problem. It looks like to me that you are not ever going to get these farmers. These farmers, you are right, they are making about a dollar off this deal, but somebody is making a whole lot more than a dollar off the deal, and those are the guys that are making the heroin. These guys are producing opium poppy, they are selling that, and it is the guys who are processing the heroin.

And I missed part of your testimony. It may be that is the target that you are onto, but it looked like to me—and I was well aware that this was a small portion of our heroin. I've been a trial judge for 20 years, so I know at least from my point of the world a little bit about this. And I knew that this was not a major source of heroin for our country, but it is for Europe and it is for Russia and it is for some other areas over there.

I asked about processing, and I didn't get a good answer. What do you—it's the heroin manufacturers, if you will, that are making the money and also the people that are shipping the finished product out of that part of the world. Where are we on attacking the manufacturers? And it's going to be our fight for a while, not theirs.

Ms. TANDY. Representative Carter, the greatest effect of my trip to Afghanistan 2 weeks ago was to recognize new opportunities for us to make headway against the stockpiles, the labs that are processing the opium into heroin, and we will be seeking to enhance our presence in Afghanistan to do that now. Until recently, security constraints in Afghanistan prevented DEA from effectively moving throughout the country. We have, as a result of my visit there, along with Assistant Secretary Charles, we have identified some new partnership opportunities to move successfully through that country. We are working with the Brits and our other partners in the country specifically to attack those labs.

I can tell you from my meetings with President Karzai, the cabinet, and the U.S. Ambassador, there is a great deal of enthusiasm in that country at all levels for going after those labs; and I am very optimistic that we will be able to make progress against the labs. We will do it in part through enhanced intelligence. I am temporarily detailing from DEA additional bodies, additional people from DEA to conduct that kind of enhanced intelligence mining with the U.S. military and assigning a person to Bagram.

We also are assigning a person to Kandahar—at least one to Kandahar to work with the Brits and other partners in Kandahar, again focused on the organizations and labs; and we are identifying trafficking organizations in that country.

We are also—we have a new country attache. We have a deputy attache, the new country attache, you may have met, who would have probably arrived in Afghanistan perhaps the same time you did.

Mr. CARTER. I think he had been there 3 days.

Ms. TANDY. His deputy will be there within 30 days. We are adding 30 more temporary detailees to the U.S. Embassy, to our office there in Afghanistan, in Kabul. So I see opportunities or I can tell you I wouldn't be pulling all of these temporary assigned people from other places in DEA and moving them into that country.

I do sense the urgency of making that progress and hitting where we will have the greatest impact, which is the labs and those organizations and doing it now.

Mr. CARTER. Absolutely. One of the things that I came away from there was that is really going to be the source of a lot of the Taliban's political opposition in this election that they are doing their best to get to. They don't have political parties. They have regional tribal influences, if you will, and the Taliban. And they have—we have them shoved down into a small area, basically there and sort of contained; and hopefully we will eventually eliminate them.

Al Qaeda, they didn't indicate to us that al Qaeda was a big player for funds. In your chart that is possible. If your chart is right, it says possible. That is kind of what they indicated to us. But it is—the warlords that are up to the north—get my direction—northeast that are trying to gain political influence are using opium poppy for that purpose.

But the bottom line is the farmer is just looking for a market for his crops. He doesn't have a market. They have had a terrible drought for 7 years. He doesn't—what little grain he produces, he doesn't have a real great market for it because of the situation over there, and he had the market with these processors for this poppy. So you can't hardly blame this poor guy—and those are poor people—for selling what he can. If we knock out the guy that is buying, then we have basically made it—it is not a cash crop anymore.

That looks like to me—and I commend you for what you are doing, and I can tell you that I came away optimistic on Afghanistan. But when you look at that place, they got major challenges over there in that country. I am optimistic because I think the President's heart is right, and I think he is really—I am very impressed with the man and the people that he has around him.

So, you know, I am very encouraged over there; and I thank you for what you are doing. Ultimately, it is going to solve the terrorist problem for this country by knocking out the drug problem.

Ms. TANDY. Thank you, Representative Carter. I share your enthusiasm and optimism and certainly the recognition of the challenges, and I thank you for your support.

Mr. CHARLES. Congressman, I just wanted to add a note of hopefulness that supports you completely.

In our meeting with President Karzai, I raised the question whether there was a political issue that we should be aware of in terms of slowing down in some way. I mean, was there anyone encouraging us to slow down on the counternarcotics effort for fear that it would have some political effect? We got the exact reverse, a firm statement that in no way was any concern going to register with him in terms of slowing down the counternarcotics effort. He was full bore on it.

I also wanted to note that, with respect to specifics—and I completely support what the administrator has just said, and again we are trying to support DEA in every way we can think of not only in Afghanistan but to support them from surrounding countries to do the same thing, to hit the traffickers, the labs, the stockpiles.

I would suggest that there are a couple of traffickers that we know, Bashir Norzi and Juma Khan, that, to the extent we can find ways to tackle their organizations and get at specifically the stockpiles there, I see no hesitance whatsoever in trying to do that.

I would also note that, on alternative development—and you make the point that these are poor farmers, it is true, but I would say to you that the margin that they get on the heroin crop versus wheat is—basically, they make a dollar on the heroin crop, they make maybe half that on wheat.

And there is also something that people often forget, that is that the Mullahs and a lot of the religious sentiment is not in favor of them getting deeply involved in the heroin trade. It is a survival issue right now.

If we can provide—and that is part of what my bureau does—the alternative development, working with USAID and others, if we can get that in behind the eradication effort, we will be able to provide them realistic opportunities both in income streams and begin to reinforce a culture that probably does not support ultimately a heroin economy.

Also just to note that we are all waiting for the DOD guidance. We are looking forward to it, because I think it will further support what you are describing as hitting the labs and hitting the stockpiles when they are found.

We are also sending more people in. I am sending three people in very, very shortly; and we expect to send six in October to reinforce these efforts in Kabul.

Finally—I will just end there—I think there is a lot to what you say, and we are highly supportive of the direction you are encouraging us to go.

Mr. CARTER. I realize my time is expired. Just one or two more comments.

I actually think the more we can do to eliminate the heroin trade over there the better it is going to make the political situation in Afghanistan, not the other way. I think that it becomes a player in these elections through these warlords and the Taliban.

Also, I want to say, we flew the highway; and they are—that is—we are to be very commended for that highway. It has changed the nature of a lot of peoples lives in the central part of Afghanistan, and that—you are to be commended for that. That is a good-looking highway, and you can—we saw a lot of traffic on the highway. I understand it has reduced the trip from Kabul to wherever it goes by—like from a day and a half to 6 hours. That has to make someone happy. So we are doing good work over there.

Mr. CHARLES. Congressman, you gave us the money to do that.

Mr. CARTER. You are doing good work. Thank you.

Mr. SOUDER. Thank you. I wanted to do some followup, and Mr. Charles gave me a nice setup. Because part of my concern is the criticism coming out of Europe, including the United Nations, which is an ironic position for us, was that we were inhibiting efforts to go after the heroin trade and were in fact sitting on it for other reasons.

You referred to the fact that you hadn't seen the Department of Defense guidance. Supposedly people on the Hill have been told that there is a policy of the Department of Defense for discovering poppy fields, labs, warehouses and drug shipments and that they have a policy of engagement in narcotics in southeast Asia.

You say that you haven't seen that—at the State Department, at least. You haven't as the person in charge of narcotics. I wondered, Ms. Tandy, have you seen a particular document from the State Department, a strategy of engagement?

Ms. TANDY. I have seen a document from the Department of Defense. I am not sure that it is a document that is being translated to the theater of operations in southwest Asia. I am just not sure if it was a concept document or if it was actual direction.

But the Department of Defense has certainly discussed guidance regarding the labs and how the labs are to be treated by military when they come upon the labs in the country. I am encouraged by what I read in the document, without getting into the direction if that is what it was in the document.

Mr. CHARLES. If I can add, yesterday I had a conversation with senior folks at DOD; and I think we are definitely experiencing forward progress, the shift from counterterrorism to counternarcotics and an understanding that if we have a little additional effort, the opportunity to hit these labs or to hit those stockpiles, they will do that.

I will also mention that I took a minute to talk with some of the Marines on the ground in Kabul just to ask them if they had the opportunity, if the guidance—which I think is in draft form now and will find its way, I have no doubt, shortly to the field, if they would—how they felt about that. I will tell you that the response was enthusiastically that they would like to execute on guidance of that sort, that there would be no hesitancy at all.

So I think we are on the right course. I think it is simply a matter of sequencing.

They were warfighting, catching terrorists. They are still doing that. This is something that we would just ask—we are all working together to try to get, as you suggest, Congressman—toward greater and greater destruction of the lab, therefore, the node, therefore, you disincentive the growth of the heroin, therefore, you create a stable and noncorrupt democracy.

Ms. TANDY. Chairman Souder, if I could add to that with regard to the Department of Defense, I have seen from the Department of Defense a real spirit of trying to see where they can meet their mission and work with the Drug Enforcement Administration in new ways; and among those—clearly, they are—these are recent developments.

The Drug Enforcement Administration has been meeting with DOD, with State Department, to try to determine where we can enhance our collaboration together. To that end, the Department of Defense has made it possible for us to put a DEA analyst into Bagram, has opened up for us the opportunity to mine the military intelligence on drugs in Bagram.

They also, in Kandahar, have offered to us the opportunity to put an agent in Kandahar for the purposes of essentially working with those returning military men and women who have been out in country, who have seen some of these labs or stockpiles, and essentially conduct after-action intelligence before those labs and stockpiles are destroyed.

What is important to DEA is not only the destruction of those labs but equally critically that we get the intelligence and information contained in those locations and working with the military in Kandahar for the after-action piece of this before the destruction will foster both of our aims in that regard. We also have been given the opportunity from DOD to interview the detainees from the dhows that were seized in the Gulf earlier this year, and we are putting together teams now. We have interviewed some of those detainees that were not in Afghanistan but elsewhere, and we are now putting teams together to—both DEA and we have invited the FBI to join us, and they will, to conduct additional interviews of the remaining detainees from the dhows.

So I do see some clearly enhanced focus in this area and a great deal of collaboration by the Department of Defense. At the same time, the DEA is enhancing its operations in Afghanistan.

Mr. SOUDER. Thank you. I appreciate the specific details of that. Part of our job in this committee and the Government Reform Committee in general is to make sure that our agencies cooperate. And that we don't have like four different nations in there simultaneously; the Nation of DEA, the Nation of the State Department, the Nation of the Department of Defense, and the Nation of the CIA, sharing that intelligence and coordinating on the ground and having a joint understanding that the military might be going after the terrorists. But the terrorists are at least in part getting their money from the narcotics; and, by the way, at the very least the weapons they are shooting at you were probably paid for, since that is a big part of the elicit economy, not by growing wheat but by growing opium poppy. If your helicopter is getting shot at, it has probably been paid for by some kind of rifle on the ground that was from the illicit economy.

Kind of understanding that we are all on the same page here, to differing degrees and priority, let me followup. It sounds like you have put additional people in the region and you are putting additional people in the region, so I have a two-part question with this.

My understanding is in Pakistan we have had a reduction from pre-September 11, from five to six agents and two intelligence analysts to now three total. Is Pakistan going to be changed as well in the total region? Do you see DEA either getting additional dollars or ramping up your presence? And do you—if you got additional dollars beyond the President's budget request, would you put them in that zone, or are there other zones in the world that have similar pressures, Colombia, for example, domestic, as every Congressman wants more DEA people in his district, including me, that—so we are all putting that domestic pressure on. But do you see this as a place where, if you got additional funding, it would be one of your priorities?

Last, on the language, when you put people, particularly if they get outside of Kabul, sounds like a lot of the time is going to be deprogramming our own military guys and their drug intelligence to build an intelligence base. But, ultimately, we all know to find the labs, to find the distribution systems, you have to penetrate organizations, which is partly buying the way in and training people from those countries. But also means you have to be able to talk to them.

Do we have an active effort—understanding that, as we have heard today, this Afghanistan effort is not likely to be over in, say, 3 months, it is not even likely to be over in 12 or 24 months, are we training people? Do we have adequate people that we can put into this zone?

I mean, let me reinforce one other thing, because I am kind of throwing this, but it is all kind of together.

Meeting with the Afghanistan ambassador to the United States the other day, in talking and trying to figure out a question we had been discussing earlier in the day about whether any of this is moving through China and replacing some of the Golden Triangle. Basically the response was those would be new routes to work through China. Yes, we could probably do it, but it is so easy right now to move through the "stans," and it is so easy to move through Turkey, they don't need to find new routes. The old routes are working fine.

The question is, are we preparing—even if we ramp up DEA, do we have people who can work undercover, who can break into these often very closed societies? And what are some of the challenges you are looking at with that?

Ms. TANDY. Chairman Souder, with regard to our ability to work undercover, develop the sources that we need beyond debriefing returning military forces and mining the military intelligence, we have not in the past been able to do that as effectively as I see our opportunities now. Part of that is because, essentially, we are confined to the bunkered quarters of the U.S. Embassy within Kabul and with really an inability to move around due to the lack of sufficient security.

That picture is changing for us. We have, even despite those obstacles, during the past year in Kabul been able to develop sources through our work within the country with a variety of partners. I see that—while we have developed some sources, I see that improving immeasurably as we are about to be able to move around within the country.

You are right. That is essential to penetrate the organizations. It is essential for us to gather our own intelligence and to combine that with what other information has been obtained by our coalition partners, our military partners and others. So I am actually quite optimistic that we are going to see a much clearer intelligence picture and that DEA will be able to conduct more traditional intelligence gathering than we do on our investigations.

With regard to the funding priorities, there is a—we have within DEA really done a scrub of all our placement of agents and analysts and staff positions around the world to determine whether where they were placed originally still makes sense today as compared to the threat, and where the threat picture changes do we need to shift some of our existing resources in the world to new places? That has resulted in what is referred to as a right-sizing proposal, which is a request that is pending before our Appropriations Committee.

I understand that is—it looks like that will be moving very shortly in a favorable way. In that proposal, we have sought the movement of a number of positions into the southwest Asian region to support Operation Containment.

As I said, the enhanced staffing for our efforts, our new efforts in Afghanistan are essentially coming from borrowing from existing positions elsewhere and detailing those into the country. The two people I mentioned, the attache and the deputy in Kabul, are permanent positions.

We originally sought a total of six positions for the country; and because of security when the office was created, we were only able to staff it with two. Now we will be able to get up to the six, but we are borrowing from other existing sources to do that.

So, to answer your question, we are streamlining our resource needs so that we match our resources to the current threat all around the world; and if additional funding is provided, clearly because I am borrowing to supply the necessary staffing to this region, those positions, a number of those positions would go to this region.

We also have positions in Pakistan that we were not able—that we are not able to fill currently. There are six of them in Pakistan. They are important. But we have not been able to fill those because of security issues in Pakistan, which leads me to a prior question that you posed, that Assistant Secretary Charles answered, that I would like to address as well, and that is our relationship between the Drug Enforcement Administration and INL.

We have a very close working relationship. Obviously, in the embassies it is the NAS officer and DEA who are trying to work through DEA's funding means within the country to effectively combat the narcotics in any given country.

I have spoken directly with Assistant Secretary Charles about some of our funding request issues. He has been responsive. He has been focused on DEA's needs to effectively combat counternarcotics, certainly in southwest Asia, certainly in Afghanistan, as well as the rest of DEA's presence around the world.

I am very pleased with our working relationship and optimistic that our funding needs will receive the kind of attention from INL and certainly from Assistant Secretary Charles that DEA has been hoping for and is seeing.

Mr. SOUDER. One of the problems when you detail people to a project like Operation Containment is that there is a lot of movement, and you don't get the people who are getting anchored into their countries who built and developed the sources over time.

Many times when I talk to agents in South America, even if they haven't been in Colombia the whole time, they have been in adjacent countries, they have built up an expertise in network and kind of know the enemy. Do you see longer times of service or building in people? I know it is a tough place to serve. But if we don't build that network of DEA agents with experience there, I am not sure we will ever penetrate.

Ms. TANDY. Chairman Souder, DEA has some of the most courageous men and women who serve under the harshest circumstances. In the last month alone, I have had agents ambushed, shot at, and engaged in a gun battle in Haiti. I have had agents approached and almost the subject of home invasions in other countries and evacuated them.

We are often serving in harsh conditions with great moral courage. And it is not the living conditions in Afghanistan. It was really having the ability to move around effectively within that country, which requires phenomenal security arrangements.

With regard to your concern about the lack of in-depth appreciation for the country situation as a detailee, I understand completely your concern in that regard. It would not be my preference to have detailees, but that is the only way that I can get resources into that country quickly.

As I said before, I see, feel, and sense a great urgency for us to get on the ground there now that we can move around and to move forward; and the only way I can meet that need is to do it with—four out of the six are detailees, two are permanent.

The need for the kind of permanent resource commitment, and understanding and appreciation for the country situation in DEA's enforcement efforts there will have to come through a traditional approval process that will take some time to work its way through, both in terms of—within the administration and the State Department; and the next stop would be, obviously, through OMB and ultimately to the Hill. Those stops take a little time. So this is my immediate approach to addressing our needs, with that longer range funding picture to go through the appropriate procedures.

Mr. SOUDER. Thank you. I am going to come back with some more questions to you.

I want to yield to Mr. Cummings.

Mr. CUMMINGS. I want to go back to this whole issue of training the police. You know, we have had a situation—I mean, this committee—subcommittee has heard testimony with regard to Mexico and how we had people even in high positions who were corrupt. And when you have—when you are dealing—with regard to drugs and folks accepting bribes.

It seems like, you know, if you think about Afghanistan, basically you are talking about a country being reborn. It seems to me that I am sure you have a lot of people who want to see their country do well, probably the vast majority. But you also have—I don't know how much these policemen are paid. How much are they paid? I mean, compared to—I know it is relative, but compared to other folks in Afghanistan.

Mr. CHARLES. I will get you an exact wage. But I will tell you that they are not well paid. I mean, they are well paid from Afghan standards, but they are going to be subject to the same pressures that law enforcement anywhere else in the world is subject to in terms of the power of drug money.

Mr. CUMMINGS. Do you think that because—I mean, do you think that because it is, again, a country being basically reborn, is that—do you think that helps to prevent some of that corruption or does—and you can look at it from a whole other angle and say, well, this is a new country. So people believing that there is discord, believing that we are still trying to get administrator, prosecution, and judges right, they might say, well, then they have these folks who are in the drug world saying, look, you know, the risk is not that bad. I mean, do you all—how do you deal with that? I mean, do you all see that as a problem?

Mr. CHARLES. Let me give you what State does, and let me give you my analogy of a gut sense of an answer to that question; and with respect to Congressman Souder's question, as with respect to yours, I am going to speak more bluntly than probably most people do.

I recently spent time also in Baghdad. I spent more time with the recruits there than I got to, given the time I had in Kabul. We are just coming off the ground. There are about 3,000 trained police in Kabal, an additional 1,400 that the Germans have trained, and we are shooting for 20,000 again by June.

But, by way of analogy, I talked a little about the whole notion of what it means in Baghdad to folks who are also going through police training, young people coming through to become professional police officers in an environment and in a culture where you are simultaneously teaching the culture at the same time and trying to empower them to make fullest use of their freedom and to preserve it against the onslaught of drug money as well as terrorism.

I was amazed at the enthusiasm of these young police officers. I found that—I asked, are you learning? And I got lectures back about how democracy works. I was being told about what they foresaw for the future of their country. I find while there are a number of factors that are different among and between the countries, I think you find that you are absolutely right. Afghanistan is in a moment of rebirth; and in that there is a sense of enthusiasm, despite poverty, despite the odds that lie out there against them.

I guess I would say to you that I hope, because the training also includes this component, that the notion of professionalism and of standing their ground for noble reasons, as long as they have the right weapons and they have the right training and they have the right protection and they have the right sense of esprit d' corps, we will stand with them.

I will tell you, I don't think there is any country on the face of the globe that doesn't face this threat, the power of drug money. I think that we have to be duly on guard. But, you know, we are actually trying to develop a way to monitor the professional futures of these people.

I was just talking back at the Department with someone about how we can monitor these people over an extended period, give them added training, give them new specialized training as they may need it, and reinforce them in time.

So the answer to the question is, we don't know yet. But I will tell you that what I have heard from the ground and from people who are in contact with those trainees is a sense of optimism.

Mr. CUMMINGS. Administrator, do we—can we trace this drug money? I mean, do we have a pretty good idea that it is going to terrorist organizations, a sizable amount of it? Can we actually trace that?

You may have answered this while I was out of the room. I don't know.

Ms. TANDY. No, actually I didn't get that question, but it is a good question. We cannot trace that yet. What I have found is that we need to do much more on the drug money front in terms of investigating it to determine those links, to trace the money, to stop the money, to seize the money, and share it with those countries that help us.

With the situation that we have here in terms of drug money in the United States is that $65 billion in U.S. dollars changes hands for drugs in the United States every single year. All law enforcement, local, State, Federal, combined, takes out less than $1 billion out of that $65.

We are, in DEA, in a hard press, attacking the drug money side in a way that we have not done in a long time. I have established in headquarters a new operation, a new office section to attack the drug money side. Every division now has drug money units in it within DEA. We are devoting resources to doing exactly what you have asked about, which is, are we tracing that drug money?

I have a management review team that is leaving on Saturday for southwest Asia, both on the drugs and the money side, to determine what more we can do in that region to answer your question, to establish these links and trace that flow of the money from heroin in the region. They will be there reviewing the entire region, Afghanistan, and the entire region of southwest Asia to determine how we can step up our efforts on the money side.

Mr. CUMMINGS. Just a last question. The chairman and I guess our entire committee, when we began to form the homeland security department, particularly after September 11, and all of our concerns that came out of that horrific event, one of our biggest concerns was whether we would—because we were so busy trying to fight terrorism, whether the fighting of drugs and other crime—in your instance drugs—would be diminished. In other words, that it would be—that because our emphasis was so—that we wanted to make sure that another September 11 never happened again.

I was just wondering—you know, I just heard you talk about borrowing, and I was just wondering, do you feel that you have—that you have enough to do what you have to do? I know Mr. Charles is sitting right there, and I know you have said some very kind things, but he is the kind of guy who can take a punch. But I was just wondering, because this is something that really concerns us.

You know, in my neighborhood, they don't worry so much about terrorists over in Afghanistan and other places. They worry about terrorists right in their neighborhoods. They have terrorists every day. They can't even come out of their houses. They hate to come home, because they don't know what drug addict has broken into their house before. So they are literally terrorized every day, and they feel it.

So I was just wondering, do you feel comfortable—and, by the way, congratulations to both of you—with your situation?

Ms. TANDY. I do. The administration and the Congress have been very generous with DEA. The administration has sought additional agent positions for DEA. We received, as a result, 216 new positions for 2003. We received another 300 plus in this latest omnibus appropriations bill that was passed. And we are scheduling—we are hiring and we are scheduling training, basic agent training, as many classes as we can accommodate at our training facility as fast as we can do them.

But that takes time to staff up, to hire. It is a 16-week training course that basic agents go through. That is after the very rigorous hiring selection process. I will tell you I do have a hiring preference for those with financial background, to again beef up what we are doing on the money side.

So we will get there. It just takes some time. We do have funding and positions to do that, but it is just going to take some time to get there.

When I talked about borrowing positions, it is really more from the standpoint of the approval process and just the natural length of time that is required to get through the various stages of approval to move permanent positions into place. So the borrowing is really more addressed to the short, immediate term while we go through the longer term process.

Mr. CUMMINGS. Thank you very much.

Mr. CHARLES. If I can add a quick footnote to that, and that is, Congressman, you don't hear very often stories in the Federal Government of people and organizations that work together effectively; and, frankly, having been an oversight guy, I made a lot of the effort to point out when that didn't happen. I can give you concrete examples here where DEA and State I think are working together in some ways better than they have ever worked together. We are about to help them, DEA, work through, organize and pay for a big conference in Peru dedicated to the internal and DEA sides working together on regional counterdrug issues. We are working collectively or together on an initiative that relates to Mexico, and it involves dollars.

By way of example,and I am going to break some glass here, very often I actually wade back in on embassies, because I think that is my job, to say DEA needs to get into the field. They are making a bona fide statement that they cannot prowl the corridors and get the information they need. They need to be out in the field, so I want you to work with them to help them get out in the field.

Dollar for dollar, I think there is an enormous amount of cooperation here, and a good example is I pulse from the reverse universe. I go back to what they call NAS officers, who are the narcotics affairs section people in these embassies who are working for State, and I say, what is your relationship with DEA? How is it working? And they are coming back with better answers than I ever heard when I was asking those questions before.

Mr. SOUDER. Before yielding to another drug warrior, Mr. Ruppersberger, who usually asks this question and probably will followup on what we just started here, which is really great to have two colleagues from the other side of the aisle really pushing us on the drug way, to say do we have adequate resources, I want to point out that Director Tandy did say that if she got additional funds that more of these positions could be permanent and there would have to be less borrowing. And that we are likely—while no administration that I have ever met goes to Congress and says, yes, my President's budget is insufficient, nevertheless, we can certainly find—if we found more money, how would you use it and what things can be done? Then we as the appropriating branch can help address that.

With that, I would like to yield to Mr. Ruppersberger.

Mr. RUPPERSBERGER. I want to make a couple of statements, and I will try to bring them into questions.

First, just as Congressman Cummings was talking about as far as the drug interdiction generally, my concern with all of the resources that we are putting into terrorism, as we should, and then the war in Iraq and Afghanistan, that is something that we have to deal with. But I am concerned about the resources, both on a Federal, State and local level, whether—if you look at the big picture right now, drugs are still the—probably the worst issue we deal with in our society. I think 90 percent of all violent crime is still drug related.

Now our job here in this committee and in Congress is to try to oversee and provide resources; and some of the things that I have seen just—specifically just with DEA, the Afghan situation is a very difficult situation. I was also just last week in both Baghdad and Afghanistan and met with Karzai. When did you meet with Karzai?

Ms. TANDY. Two weeks ago.

Mr. RUPPERSBERGER. Well, this was last week; and that country has a long way to go. The infrastructure—I mean, the fact that they were under different control with Russia and everything else. My concern is that Karzai is still around. Because, as you saw, if you met with him, he has tremendous security. And when we—and he does—I think one of the reasons, and I hope that he wins his election, is because he has relationships with the warlords and with other people in the country.

When we talked with him about the issue of what is happening with heroin again, his concern was that he knows it is a problem. It undermines his ability just to create an economy for jobs. Because the money is just coming in as far as heroin is concerned.

But my thought, after I left there, it is going to take a long time, and we are going to have to have a lot of patience to deal with the issue of turning these warlords and farmers and taking that product—and whether it is eradication, but then you have to put something else in there. With all of the political issues that are there, it is going to be difficult.

I think the way we get in, though, is our fight against terrorism. Because we know that a lot of money and focus is going in that arena.

By the way, Secretary Charles, I would agree with you also on the teamwork approach. Both being in Afghanistan and Iraq and some other countries, I have never seen the teamwork in all of the different agencies coming together. I mean, from the CIA to the military to the DEA, the Secretary—I mean, it is all coming together, and there is one focus.

The only way we get out of those countries, though, is to train their police officers and their defense for security. We had our delegation. There were six of us from the Intelligence Committee; and we made sure, even though they didn't want us to go out into the red zone, that we went and laid a wreath on behalf of those 23 police officers in Baghdad that were killed.

Because the strategy has changed—and you probably are aware of this—that they are not only going after our coalition, the United States and Great Britain, but also they are trying to put the pressure and kill and do whatever they can to these police officers.

We probably had about 300 people in the academy in Iraq, and these individuals were so happy that we were there they put their hands over their hearts. I think that the insurgents, along with the outside al Qaeda groups that are now, say, just in Baghdad and also in Afghanistan, they are making a mistake. Because when they start killing Iraqis, Iraqis are getting upset about it. Their resolve is strong.

Now let's get to some questions.

First thing, I think one of the things with Afghanistan, is that the good news for the United States is that almost all of the heroin from Afghanistan is going to European countries. I think most of ours comes from Mexico and Colombia. Am I correct?

By the way, Colombia is an example of us training Colombians to take care of their own problem. They are getting a lot stronger. They are getting better results.

I heard over there, because I asked questions about the issue of drugs, that Great Britain and other countries could probably do more than they are doing to work with us to help their problem. It is more of their problem than our problem right now. How would you respond to that?

Mr. CHARLES. Well, let me say we discussed this briefly earlier. I think that what we are doing, what I am doing personally—and I have engaged with them both on U.S. soil and abroad, particularly on Afghanistan, to try to get them to—all of us to work together in a more aggressive approach. Let me say that there are things that the British are doing that they are doing exceedingly well, some of which we can't talk about in this room. There are other things that we could be doing a lot better together on.

As you probably know, in Afghanistan, the counternarcotics piece is being worked with the British, the police training piece is with the Germans, and the justice sector reform and the building of courthouses and the training is being worked with the Italians. One of my priorities is to bring them more on board and have us drive harder at the target.

Mr. RUPPERSBERGER. Because I saw that as an issue, that we need—I mean, the Europeans are the victims of Afghanistan right now more than we are, would you agree? Other than the issue of money and terrorism.

Mr. CHARLES. I do agree.

Mr. SOUDER. Supplemental to his question, because you put a specific dollar amount on Britain before, do you have a dollar amount for the Germans or French and other European countries?

Mr. CHARLES. Yes. One of the things that this—one of the charts that I have here is strictly counternarcotics. I can get you the other ones as they relate to justice and to police training. The Germans are being very—I think very cooperative and very aggressive. In fact, so are the Italians.

Mr. RUPPERSBERGER. How about the French?

Mr. CHARLES. Yes. It is a varying—everybody contributes what they can contribute. Or that has sort of been the history up to this point.

One of the things that I am suggesting and pushing is that people contribute more and we drive harder at these targets.

Now in the justice sector component, it is a smaller overall piece. In other words, $10 million we are driving at the justice sector. So the Italian piece relative to that might be proportionally more but dollars less.

The police training piece we are pushing very hard for. That is a dollar-intensive effort. But let me say to date we have trained again about 3,000, they have trained about 1,400. There is a concerted effort to ramp up on both sides. So far as I can tell, we are working closely together. I talked to them briefly in Madrid about that when we were on another topic.

But let me just give you some numbers. I gave you the U.K. numbers, and those are fairly large. But Australia, we have $261,000; France, $230,000; Italy, $1.6 million; Canada, $165,000; Germany was $365,000. We also have Canada, Ireland, Japan, Austria, Netherlands. What I am telling you is this is definitely a mutual effort.

Mr. RUPPERSBERGER. The good news I saw with Afghanistan versus Iraq is we have more coalition in Afghanistan. That shares the load, including putting our own people at risk, too.

Mr. CHARLES. That is right.

Mr. RUPPERSBERGER. I see the red light.

The political situation has to be resolved. They are talking about elections and whatever in Afghanistan. I don't see this production situation in Afghanistan alleviating itself for a long period of time, because the first thing you have to get the political control, the security and whatever.

Two things I want to say. First thing, what would our more long-term goal be to deal with the Afghan heroin issue? I know eradication and all of those issues, but I think if you raise expectations and you don't make them, that is even worse. So we have to be realistic.

Second, I am just concerned again that we take—that we don't take our eye off the ball in Colombia and Mexico, Burma, some of these other hot spots that we know that we have to deal with, also. We are focusing a lot on terrorism, but there is a lot that is happening in other parts that if we don't keep our eye on the ball in some of those other hotspots—South America is a perfect example. If we don't keep our eye on the ball, are we OK globally? Because I think if you talk to most agencies throughout the world, including intelligence agencies, they will tell you that most of the focus now is over in the Iraq and the Afghan area.

Mr. CHARLES. Why don't we both give you an answer? I know the administrator has something to say, also.

Ms. TANDY. On the long term—in the short and long term on the enforcement side of that, I can tell you where the focus is. It is to attack the stockpiles, the labs, go after the key trafficking organizations, both in the region and——

Mr. RUPPERSBERGER. Is this long term in the whole world or just Afghanistan?

Ms. TANDY. I am talking both in the region—in southwest Asia as well as within Afghanistan. We are identifying what has commonly been referred to in the past as kingpins. We are identifying trafficking organizations within——

Mr. RUPPERSBERGER. Not the farmers as much, the traffickers once they are getting—that really——

Ms. TANDY. Trafficking organizations.

Mr. RUPPERSBERGER. Follow the money.

Ms. TANDY. Yes, and in terms of the region as well, those that are transporting and trafficking, both in terms of the drugs and the chemicals that are being used at the labs to actually process the opium into heroin, the long-term piece of that has already started now, and we are working closely with our British counterparts in the country.

On the enforcement side, the U.K. has been a very strong leader, and DEA has a very strong partnership with the Brits in attacking these areas of the counternarcotics issue.

Regionally for us, it is Operation Containment until INL and the coalition pieces come together in terms of standing up a real police force and standing up prosecutors and judges and prisons to effectively house traffickers at this level. It is Operation Containment attacking in the surrounding countries the flow of heroin and the money and the chemicals out of Afghanistan that is going to further cement our enforcement success in that region over the long term and the short term.

Mr. RUPPERSBERGER. But are we taking resources away from what affects the U.S.A., the Mexico and the Colombia area? I mean, that is what worries me.

Ms. TANDY. I can tell you for the Drug Enforcement Administration we are not taking any resources away from Colombia and Mexico.

Mr. RUPPERSBERGER. That is good to hear.

Ms. TANDY. We have a right-sizing proposal that I mentioned earlier in my testimony that actually enhances our position in those countries.

With regard to the source heroin, source countries for the United States which you asked about during your opening statement, it is Colombia, by and far the largest heroin supply source for the United States, at about 80 percent. Afghanistan, the southwest Asian region is No. 2, with Mexico closely on the heels of that. And southeast Asia——

Mr. RUPPERSBERGER. Coming to the United States?

Ms. TANDY. Coming to the United States.

Mr. RUPPERSBERGER. It is Afghanistan No. 2?

Ms. TANDY. Well, we can't isolate it out as Afghanistan.

Mr. RUPPERSBERGER. Because all of the documents I have read and research, including a lot that I have over there, said the opposite, that the two major areas were—in the briefing information—were Mexico and Colombia for the United States, and Afghanistan was all of the European areas but not the United States.

Ms. TANDY. Well, I can tell you that from our programs within DEA testing the signature of heroin coming into this country to determine its regional source as well as the purchase of domestic samples of heroin and determining where that is coming from geographically, what we have seen is that the No. 2 is Afghanistan, excuse me—southwest Asia, to include Afghanistan.

Mr. RUPPERSBERGER. Could you get me that information? Because I tell you, we have a committee that was getting briefed to the contrary; and I will get the documents. I would like to see that because we got to get our facts straight if we are talking about helping and authorizing.

Ms. TANDY. I think part of the confusion is that there is only a hair worth of difference between southwest Asia as a source and the volume coming out of Mexico. It is a percentage point at best difference between the two.

The actual numbers we are not going to have until September when we finish analyzing the samples from those two programs to further isolate precisely where that standing is. But I will be delighted to give you the information we do have to date.

Mr. RUPPERSBERGER. I will try to get you a copy of that briefing so you will see what we had.

Mr. CHARLES. Congressman, if I can respond to your long-term versus short-storm and long-term overall strategy. In Afghanistan, the strategy, as it should be and as it is all over the world, is to put these countries in the driver's seat as democracies controlling their own problems and ultimately bringing them down to a manageable level so that we back out. We have helped them to create the democracy, to stabilize the environment, to knock out the drug trade, to wring it out, if you will, from the democratic process, so that it doesn't infect the process.

The same is true in Colombia. I can guarantee you that we are not diverting anything. In fact, quite the reverse. We have an Indian region initiative that we will talk about at some other future date in which we are spending about $1 billion very directly on stabilizing, regionalizing and ultimately creating more of a drug-free environment there.

We fly against the crops there. We are building judicial institutions there. We are doing many, many things there, also supportive of domestic law enforcement there.

In Afghanistan, in Iraq—and you mentioned Iraq for stabilization. We have $800 million dedicated to the proposition of this bureau, to the proposition of training the police. We are it in Jordan, and we just built that academy, and we are doing it also in Baghdad. That academy that you were at is actually managed by INL with MPs also teaching there.

In Afghanistan, the end game is similar. It is freedom, it is democracy, it is a self-administered set of programs.

But the thing I think that is important to keep in mind is—and this is where in many ways you are seeing both halves of the canoe here to get us across the lake—the law enforcement community, the U.S. law enforcement community, which is what the administrator has been talking about, throws the pitch out to the field. There also has to be a catcher out there somewhere. That is what we do. We help the countries to be able to absorb, interact, have a high-integrity law enforcement community that they can interface with.

One example that I feel it is important to give, because it was asked by the chairman a moment ago, in terms of the support and containment strategy, is there any good news, bad news in the ability to execute this from the catcher's point of view, from the working-in-these-countries' point of view. I will tell you the bad news is, as it relates to Afghanistan, is that there is very little law enforcement capacity in these countries that surround Afghanistan, arranging broadly. Therefore, every effort, whether it is intelligence sharing, whether it is execution of finding things and destroying them or running down traffickers or prosecuting them, all of that is something we are building right now. The anticorruption efforts, all of these fit together like pieces in a jigsaw puzzle. We are desperately trying in each of those countries to ramp that up. Since I have been there, it has become, I think, an added priority.

In Pakistan, though—because I think I don't want to leave you with a wrong impression. In Pakistan, I think we are getting significant cooperation; and I want to tell you how significant. We fly a number of aircraft in there in support of—or we have them being utilized with the antinarcotics police that work in Afghanistan—in Pakistan. They have been conducting aerial surveillance. They have been working on counterterrorism activities, doing medivacs, rescue operations all related to the border. We have antinarcotics forces in—the antinarcotic force in Badakhshan has increased operations 60 percent over 2002.

Nationwide, heroin seizures on INL-supported programs are 224 percent up. Opium seizures are up 125 percent; 63 percent increase in seizures in Badakhshan itself. We talked about the road earlier, 431 kilometers, which allows law enforcement, antiterrorism forces, antinarcotics forces to actually get into country.

We have 80,000 acceptable 10-print finger cards which gives us a program that didn't exist before. Pakistan has destroyed 4,200 hectares of opium poppy in 2003.

So there are certainly positive pieces of news as it relates to the countries surrounding Afghanistan. But the issue is a big one. I would just tell you on the dollar side, the question about could more be done, the answer is, I think this is—these are all locations in which more could be done.

I think that the one thing to keep our eye on is it is not as if something shifting from one priority to another, from one region to another. It is the fact that—I think you put your finger on it, Congressman—that counternarcotics in these places has the potential to disrupt democracy, to fund terrorism, and to ultimately diminish the security that we have back here.

We lose, as the administrator I think alluded to earlier, thousands last year, I think the CDC said 21,000 young Americans died at the hands of drugs. We cannot afford that kind of an effect in this country. That is why we have to be so aggressive abroad in trying to turn the clock back and get this back, roll it back.

Mr. RUPPERSBERGER. OK. Good.

Mr. SOUDER. Thank you.

I want to say for the record that on Tuesday we are having a hearing on the Andean region, and the Department of Defense will be here, in addition to the Colombia—focused on Colombia, but also Peru, Bolivia and Ecuador.

Because, as you heard from a number of us today, we are all very concerned about Afghanistan. We're all very concerned about Iraq, for multiple reasons, and particularly the heroin problem, that 7 to 10 percent coming into our United States. But we don't really know from all of the signature problems precisely what is doing it. Obviously, if Europe didn't get the Afghan heroin, we would see another explosion out of the Indian region, because that market would also increasingly supply Europe.

We have the interconnections that we need to—but we don't want to forget both our domestic and our Andean area which is—that and Mexico are the primary suppliers to us. So our committee will stay focused on those areas even as we do this.

I wanted to make sure, because I probed a little bit with Director Tandy, but I wanted to ask Mr. Charles, too, that if you had another hundred million, would you be able to use it in this region? Also, precisely what did you mean in your testimony when you said that you reprogrammed $50 million for accelerating success in Afghanistan? Where did that come from?

Mr. CHARLES. Let me answer the second one first, and then—that $50 million actually that I was talking about was the supplemental. The $170 million that I indicated was actually for police and justice sector programs in Afghanistan. The $50 million is what the U.S. Congress gave us.

Mr. SOUDER. So when your testimony says, to which the administration added $50 million in reprogrammed funds, that didn't necessarily come from your department. That could have come from other parts of the government?

Mr. CHARLES. I will get back to you, but I think it was supplemental funding. I don't think it was reprogrammed away from another area, but I will come back to you on that.

The answer to your question about what would you do with an additional $100 million, we are not asking for more money right now. But I would tell you that there are parts of the world in which that money could be highly—if you said regionally what would you do with it, I would put immediately $40 million of it directly into Afghanistan right now.

We are driving hard on the eradication piece, but, as the other Congressmen have indicated, it is necessarily targeted. We are only going to be able to hit—and I want to keep expectations at this level—10 to 15 percent of the overall crop this year. That will send a strong signal, but you can do more. You can also do more, I think, on information sharing, and there are a number of other areas. So I would probably put $40 million of the hundred there.

In Pakistan, we have a crying need for some additional—I think it could be absorbed, let's put it that way—an additional $40 million probably.

Then with the remainder, I think probably southeast and southwest Asia are critically important areas. Turkey is a critically important area. There is no question that I think we can do more in each of those areas. If the question is, could it be absorbed, the answer is, absolutely, it could be absorbed.

I also want to note that very often in this we get in the mindset or the impression that somehow we are just sitting in place spinning our wheels against a problem that continues to blow at us, and we are never going to go forward. I take a very different point of view. I am absolutely committed to the idea that in each of these places, Afghanistan and Colombia in particular, there is a real end game and that real end game relates to both counterterrorism and counternarcotics, and you get them down to a level where it is manageable indigenously and with multilateral international support as and when needed.

I think one of the things that we forget is—I was in conversation just yesterday with an ambassador from a foreign country, and I was trying to explain that in this country there was a fellow by the name of Elliott Ness. He took a long, hard view at Al Capone and organized crime in this country, and he went after them with all of his heart, and he helped to beat them.

That is what we are trying to do in these places, bringing crime, terrorism, narcotics down to a level in which it is manageable in the way that we manage crime elsewhere. We will never eliminate crime from Los Angeles or anywhere else in the world. We will get it down to a level where it is manageable. That is our end game in places like this.

Mr. SOUDER. I appreciate your patience with us. I have one other question, because you have been, appropriately, very cautious about the links between al Qaeda and the drug terrorism, although we have seen links with other terrorist organizations. But you had specific references in your testimony to these real major operations in Turkey where you said, in 2002, we got as much as all of—in one bust all of 2000. That, in Europe, your best evidence that you can sort through were these—because both of you stated in your testimony that we want to break this stuff up in Afghanistan and others while we are dealing with maybe regional drug lords before this really explodes again and dominates and prohibits democracy from flourishing in Afghanistan and rebuilding the country. It is what President Karzai says. It is what the former king says.

That is an extraordinary amount of money. Somebody is making a lot of profit when you have $1 billion takedown, some phenomenal number you said, on the heroin.

Ms. TANDY. In the United States, it is $65 billion a year.

Mr. SOUDER. Also, the one big bust in Turkey where you found the stockpiled stuff, were the busts in Turkey—were they just profiteering? Were they early signs of a large cartel? Were there any signs of those people being on a watch list? What type of organization is that big that they would have in one stockpile that much?

Ms. TANDY. I don't have the details at this point to provide to you. I am not sure if the investigation is still continuing there. So, with your permission, what I would like to do is get back to you with as much as I can provide to you with regard to those details.

Mr. SOUDER. I would really appreciate that.

Because one of our challenges, without disclosing too much from your agents, as our former staff director and your now employee, Chris Donesa, could testify as well, when we were in Europe we heard that one of the problems we have with organization law in Europe is that we can't follow this stuff through because you can't continue to see how the stuff moves in the finances and through the organizations. Therefore, when sometimes we take it down in Turkey or places before it gets into the distribution network, we can't see. We have assumptions that it may have been going to some of the al Qaeda networks in Europe, but they are assumptions.

We are being very cautious about what we actually say, because we have some legal problems that we have to address with Europe. If the heroin is being consumed there, you would think that they want to help us with some of this information.

But anything you can give to the committee would be appreciated. Do you have anything you want to say?

Thank you very much for your testimony and look forward to continuing to work with both of you. Thank you for your leadership, and we will continue to work on a close basis.

With that, the subcommittee stands adjourned.

[Whereupon, at 4:10 p.m., the subcommittee was adjourned.]

[The prepared statement of Hon. Tom Davis and additional information submitted for the hearing record follow:]

Statement of Chairman Tom Davis
Hearing on "Afghanistan: Law Enforcement Interdiction Efforts in Transshipment Countries to Stem the Flow of Heroin"
Subcommittee on Criminal Justice, Drug Policy and Human Resources
February 26, 2003

Last week I led a bipartisan delegation to Iraq, Pakistan and Afghanistan to ascertain our efforts in the fight against terrorism. During this trip I became painfully aware of how complex our situation has become vis-à-vis Afghanistan and how illicit narcotics help fuel the various terror networks within the region. Eliminating the illegal drug trade, primarily in the form of opium production and hashish, is a major factor in winning the war on terror. It is clear the region's illicit drug trade funds Al Qaeda, the Taliban, and the terrorist organization Hizb-I Islami Gulbuddin (HIG). If we are to win the war in Afghanistan we need to address how narcotics play a large part in funding the radical anti-western elements who are desperate for instability to continue to dominate the region.

Solving the narcotics problem in Afghanistan is no easy task. 25 years of constant war and brutal dictatorships have legitimized the drug trade. Afghani farmers, because they are in desperate need of money, plant poppies along side their food crops. This presents many social and logistical problems. Socially the Afghan farmer sees poppies much like our farmers see cotton or soybeans. Logistically aerial eradication becomes an impossible way to resolve this dilemma because poppies are planted next to food crops. Therefore, I believe the only way to solve the Afghanistan role in the drug trade is to come up with a comprehensive plan, which at its core incentivizes the farmer to not plant poppy, and disincentivizes them if they do.

A "Plan Afghanistan" needs resources, determination and leadership. The U.S. needs to take a more active role in resolving this problem. Last week the delegation I led met with INL and DEA representatives in Kabul. Their determination to address the poppy problem was evident, but they lack the resources to truly make a difference. Our resolve to restore Afghanistan's war-torn people needs to include a broad comprehensive plan to eradicate the poppy production, to not only help the people of Afghanistan but to cut off the funding of the terror organizations that threaten our security.

I would like to thank Chairman Souder for organizing today's important hearing to review the Administration's counter narcotics program in Afghanistan and the region. We have an opportunity to help the Afghan people begin a new life and simultaneously cut off the money flow to terror organizations like Al Qaeda. I look forward to hearing testimony this afternoon from the State Department and DEA on their efforts in Afghanistan and what is planned for the future.

Robert B. Charles
Committee on Government Reform
February 26, 2004
Page 37, Line 838

Question:

As reflected in the transcript, State/INL Assistant Secretary Robert B. Charles stated that he concurred with Administrator Karen Tandy that 7-10 percent of the heroin on our streets today originated in Afghanistan, or at least Southeast and Southwest Asia. Although a question was not raised specifically by a Member, a tab was placed in the transcript indicating a question.

Answer:

According to the Department of Justice's Intelligence Division, Office of Strategic Intelligence, Domestic Strategic Intelligence Unit, as of September 2004, preliminary data for 2003 indicates that 1 percent of heroin in the U.S. originated from Southeast Asia and 8 percent originated from Southwest Asia. In 2002, 1 percent of heroin in the U.S. came from Southeast Asia and 10 percent from Southwest Asia. In 2001, 7 percent of heroin in the U.S. originated from Southeast Asia and 7 percent from Southwest Asia. For the past three years, an average of 8 percent of heroin in the U.S. originated from Southwest Asia, with Afghanistan the most likely source. Afghanistan is the primary producer of opium in Southwest Asia, although Southwest Asian heroin may actually be processed in other countries in the region. Burma is the major source of Southeast Asian opium and heroin.

Robert B. Charles
Committee on Government Reform
February 26, 2004
Page 72, Line 1709

Question

As reflected in the transcript, State/INL Assistant Secretary Robert B. Charles was asked by Representative Souder to provide information regarding the amount of funding provided by the "Germans or French and other European countries" to support ongoing law enforcement efforts in Afghanistan (testimony before the House Committee on Government Reform, February 26, 2004.)

Answer:

With regard to counternarcotics efforts, the attached matrix provided to State/INL by the British Government, the lead nation on counternarcotics efforts in Afghanistan, indicates donor countries and the funding they have pledged, budgeted or appropriated. Further, based on information provided to INL by the international community during multilateral meetings on the topic of Afghanistan assistance, the following is the amount of funding pledged, budgeted, or appropriated since 2002 (in U.S. dollars, unless stated otherwise) by country for law enforcement efforts, including judiciary and police:

Australia ($1,460,000 for border and airport security);

Austria ($333,000 for justice sector and $236,500 for border security);

Belgium ($678,000 for police salaries);

Canada ($1,319,000 for justice sector; C$7,800,000 for police sector);

China ($4.5 million for police sector);

Denmark ($100,000 for police salaries);

European Union ($3,750,000 for justice sector and $88,850,000 for police sector);

Germany ($19,200,000 for police sector, and $435,000 for justice sector employees);

Iran ($1,600,000 for police border security posts);

Ireland ($735,715 for police salaries);

Italy, the lead on justice sector reform ($13,120,000 and an unspecified amount to train 44 police officers in criminal procedure law and capacity building training);

Japan, lead for Disarmament, Demobilization, and Reintegration ($12,110,000 for police sector);

Liechtenstein ($35,475 for police salaries);

Netherlands ($9,450,000 for police sector);

Norway ($4,814,100 for police sector);

Pakistan (train 1,200 police recruits and senior police officers, unspecified amount);

Qatar (hosted international conference in Doha, May 2004);

Russia (between $3 and $5 million for police equipment, vehicles, and training);

Sweden ($250,000 for justice sector);

Switzerland ($379,564 for a senior administrative police advisor and $250,000 for police salaries); and

UK ($6,252,000 for justice sector and $89,78,77,150 for police sector).

Some of these contributions are for multi-year projects requiring continued international support and donations. The U.S. and U.K. continue to encourage donor support.

Robert B. Charles
Committee on Government Reform
February 26, 2004
Page 83, Line 1983

Question:

As reflected in the transcript, State/INL Assistant Secretary Robert B. Charles was asked by Representative Souder to clarify whether the $50 million in FY 2004 funding that was provided for counternarcotics efforts in Afghanistan were reprogrammed funds or supplemental funds (testimony before the House Committee on Government Reform, February 26, 2004.) Assistant Secretary Charles indicated that he believed that these funds were supplemental funds.

Answer:

The $50 million provided to State/INL in FY 2004 were supplemental funds.

Questions for the Record Submitted to
Assistant Secretary Robert Charles by
Chairman Mark E. Souder (#1)
Subcommittee for Criminal Justice,
Drug Policy & Human Resources
Committee on Government Reform
February 26, 2004

Question:

Could you explain the benefits of and how the Flexible Rewards program would work, with respect to farmers and economic alternatives in Afghanistan? How much money does the program cost? What benefits are derived?

Answer:

The Department of State does not have a Flexible Rewards program with respect to farmers and economic alternatives in Afghanistan. Since FY 2002, however, we have been supporting alternative development programs in Afghanistan aimed at providing farmers with economically viable alternatives to the cultivation of opium poppy. Some of our funds have supported the work of non-governmental organizations with considerable experience in rural development: The Aga Khan Foundation, Relief International, Mercy Corps International and Central Asia Development Group (CADG).

The Bureau for International Narcotics and Law Enforcement Affairs (INL) received $29 million in FY02 and $5 million in FY04 Supplemental funding for alternative rural livelihoods. Benefits have included establishment of community development institutions, technology training, livestock and land development, micro-credit loans, agricultural marketing, and development of agricultural cooperatives. We have cooperated closely with USAID in the promotion of these alternative development projects. As funding permits, we expect to sustain and expand ongoing alternative development programs, particularly in areas where we are assisting efforts by the central government to eradicate opium poppy fields. We see alternative development programs as a vital element in an integrated counternarcotics effort in Afghanistan aimed at eliminating opium poppy cultivation and promoting non-opium based agricultural development.

Questions for the Record Submitted to
Assistant Secretary Robert Charles by
Chairman Mark E. Souder (#2)
Subcommittee for Criminal Justice,
Drug Policy & Human Resources
Committee on Government Reform
February 26, 2004

Question:

How are your efforts divided between Afghanistan, the Andean Region and other source countries? Which of these efforts has been most successful and why? Of your most challenged efforts, what are the issues?

Answer:

In FY 2004, INL received regular appropriation funding of $726.687 million for the Andean Counterdrug Initiative (ACI) account and $240.274 million for the International Narcotics Control and Law Enforcement (INCLE) account. In addition, INL received FY 2004 supplemental funding of $220 million for Afghanistan and $885.7 million for Iraq. Of the FY 2004 regular and supplemental amounts, approximately 88 percent supports counter-drug efforts and law enforcement developmental efforts in Afghanistan, Iraq and the Andean Region. The remaining 12 percent in funding is targeted for other country/account programs.

INL programs have matured in the two decades we have been engaged in counter-drug efforts in the Andean region. Since 1999, a little over $3 billion have been invested in the ACI countries. There have been many success stories, especially in recent years, as our investments began to bear fruit. Coca cultivation for the region decreased by 22 percent between 2001 and 2003. Current estimates for 2004 indicate that there will likely be another decrease in cultivation. Opium poppy cultivation has decreased by almost 33 percent for the region. Cocaine seizures are at an all-time high of 221 metric tons for the region in 2003, an increase of 70 percent from 2001. These seizures and eradication efforts prevented over 500 metric tons of cocaine from reaching the U.S last year. Well over a hundred-thousand families, over 1,200 child soldiers and one million displaced persons in Colombia have benefited from ACI funding and development projects in the region.

In comparison to the Andean region, INL's programs in Iraq and Afghanistan are relatively new and therefore are the most challenging. Both Iraq and Afghanistan are emerging from a wartime environment. The unsettled security situations and lack of infrastructure in both countries pose a direct challenge to effective counternarcotics and policing efforts. However, in spite of the challenges, we are achieving success with both our Afghan and Iraq police training programs.

As part of U.S. efforts to strengthen Afghan security and stability by rebuilding the national police, our assistance built and rehabilitated six Afghan police training facilities. We began by establishing a central Training Center in Kabul in May 2003. Since then, we have established five additional Regional Training Centers (RTCs) using interim facilities in Kandahar, Konduz, Mazar-i-Sharif, Gardez, and Jalalabad and trained over 26,000 police.

U.S. efforts to strengthen Iraqi security and stability include the training of the Iraq Police Service at the Jordan International Training Center near Amman, Jordan and the Baghdad Public Service Academy in Baghdad, Iraq. As of February 26, 2004, over 400 new police cadets have completed the eight-week police-training program at the Jordan International Police Training Center. In addition, 2,388 cadets are in training at the Jordan Facility and the Baghdad Public Safety Academy.

Questions for the Record Submitted to
Assistant Secretary Robert Charles by
Chairman Mark E. Souder (#3)
Subcommittee for Criminal Justice,
Drug Policy & Human Resources
Committee on Government Reform
February 26, 2004

Question:

How are land-based efforts at interception and interdiction of narcotics departing Afghanistan organized? What methods are used along the borders of Afghanistan and Pakistan, Uzbekistan and Iran to interdict trans-border shipments?

Answer:

INL has supplied 1100 vehicles, hundreds of items of communications gear, and significant amounts of surveillance equipment for border monitoring operations in Pakistan to civilian agencies, two of which, the Frontier Corps and the Anti-Narcotics Force, are operating on the western border. INL has expanded border security assistance to the Pakistani Ministry of Interior to include constructing frontier roads in the Federally Administered Tribal Areas (FATA) and supported efforts to make FATA local security officials more effective. Efforts also include upgrading the Torkham border crossing, a major port of entry along the Pakistan-Afghanistan frontier, to enhance security and immigration/customs checks. INL is also funding Frontier Corps construction of 55 outposts along Afghanistan's western border to enhance Frontier Corps' presence.

Paramilitary Frontier Corps units serving under the Ministry of Interior have primary responsibility for securing Pakistan's rugged 1500 mile-long border with Afghanistan. The Frontier Corps has approximately 30,000 personnel stationed in both Balochistan and the Northwest Frontier Province (NWFP) who can launch interdiction missions and detain suspects, and who then turn them over to the police, Anti-Narcotics Force, or Federal Investigation Agency.

To address the problem of Afghanistan traffickers causing major disruptions along its border, Iran has invested as much as $800 million in a system of berms, moats, concrete dams, sentry points and observation towers, as well as a road along its entire eastern border with Pakistan and Afghanistan. In addition, according to an Iranian Government Internet site, Iran has constructed 212 border posts, 205 observation posts, 22 concrete barriers, 290 km. of canal, 659 km. of soil embankments, a 78 km. barbed wire fence, and 2,654 km. of asphalt and gravel roads. Thirty-thousand law enforcement personnel are regularly deployed along the border.

In addition, the UN Office of Drugs and Crime (UNODC) implemented a border project in 2003 near the city of Termez, Uzbekistan, (Hayraton Bridge checkpoint) on the border with Afghanistan.

The Hayraton checkpoint is open to military traffic to and from northern Afghanistan near Mazaar al-Sharif, Afghanistan and opened to limited commercial traffic in early 2004. UNODC is developing a joint training package for border security officers from Tajikistan, Turkmenistan and Afghanistan, along with an Uzbekistan unit to commence in the last quarter of CY 2004. Such training will be an ongoing part of the project once primary construction of the customs and border checkpoint buildings is completed. Separate projects will coordinate training and equipment for several countries within the region. Training will include counternarcotics information sharing, controlled delivery operations, and computerized case management software.

Questions for the Record Submitted to
Assistant Secretary Robert Charles by
Chairman Mark E. Souder (#4)
Subcommittee for Criminal Justice, Drug Policy & Human Resources
Committee on Government Reform
February 26, 2004

Question :

We understand that there is little presence of the Pakistani central government in the Federally Administered Tribal Areas along the Afghan border, nor in Balochistan, which border Afghanistan and Iran. What is your strategy to disrupt drug smuggling routes in those lightly patrolled areas and with maritime routes like go-fast boat smuggling between Balochistan and Oman in the Persian Gulf?

Answer:

The INL-supported Border Security Program addresses the serious gaps in the Government of Pakistan's capacity to secure its western border by enabling it to conduct aerial surveillance missions and interdiction operations along the border. The program enhances the ability of law enforcement and border security forces to access, patrol, and mount interdiction operations in the remote border regions, including the Federally Administered Tribal Areas (FATA), through the construction of roads and outposts, and through the provision of commodities such as vehicles, communications gear, and surveillance equipment. The program also includes increasing the organizational and operational capacity of border forces to confront crime and terrorism through training and by improving coordination among law enforcement agencies. The Border Security Program targets border security and law enforcement forces (Frontier Corps and the Anti-Narcotics Force) operating on the border in the North West Frontier Province (NWFP)and Balochistan Provinces, as well as the FATA.

INL is also working with DOD's Office of Special Operations, Low Intensity Conflict, and Counter-Narcotics to develop a complementary border security program on the Afghan side of the border utilizing DOD's $73 million FY 2004 Supplemental for counter-narcotics programs in Afghanistan and neighboring countries. Embassy Islamabad's Narcotics Affairs Section and the Drug Enforcement Administration (DEA) participate in the South Asia Foreign Anti-Narcotics Committee, which meets monthly to share information and coordinate counter-narcotics assistance as well.

Ongoing Operation Enduring Freedom Coalition counter-terrorism efforts in the Gulf of Oman region serve as a partial deterrent to drug trafficking. Additional USG-funded programs, such as the Container Security Initiative project at the port of Karachi, will also assist in countering trafficking. The air assets we have provided to the Pakistani Ministry of Interior Air Wing have been deployed for surveillance and other missions in FATA, NWFP, Balochistan and in support of the Maritime

Security Agency Coast Guard along the Makran Coast. The Air Wing unit is the only fully capable night-vision-goggle (NVG) air unit in Pakistan. The air-ground border security information and operations will be integrated with increased intelligence sharing and coordination through a border security coordination center planned for construction in Quetta.

Questions for the Record Submitted to
Assistant Secretary Robert Charles by
Chairman Mark E. Souder (#5)
Subcommittee for Criminal Justice,
Drug Policy & Human Resources
Committee on Government Reform
February 26, 2004

Question :

Have you met with Under Secretary Hutchinson, Admiral Collins, Commissioner Bonner, Assistant Secretary Garcia or Roger Mackin to discuss counternarcotics strategies and synergies between DHS and INL?

Answer:

I have met with Admiral Collins, Roger Mackin, Under Secretary Hutchison and DEA Administrator Tandy on separate occasions to discuss counternarcotics strategies in various regions of the world. I have spoken with Admiral Loy, Commissioner Bonner and US SOUTHCOM General Hill on various issues. For example, INL and DHS closely coordinate resources and policy related to U.S.-Mexico border security issues. I participated directly with DHS Secretary Ridge and Attorney General Ashcroft in the 2003 Mexican-American Bi-national Convention. We also work closely with DHS on Andean aerial tracking and interdiction programs. Regionally, the ongoing European Union project for Border Operations Management in Central Asia (BOMCA) program leverages close collaboration between DHS' Bureau of Customs and Border Protection and

INL to support USG strategies and techniques within the European Union's multi-million euro project. In addition, INL program officers meet regularly with the DHS-sponsored Export Control and Border Security (EXBS) program at the working level.

Questions for the Record Submitted to
Assistant Secretary Robert Charles by
Chairman Mark E. Souder (#6)
Subcommittee for Criminal Justice,
Drug Policy & Human Resources
Committee on Government Reform
February 26, 2004

Question :

Could you elaborate on your perception of the commitment of the Karzai government on counternarcotics and counterterrorism?

Answer:

The Karzai government is strongly committed to combating terrorism and the drug trade. President Karzai himself has characterized the drug trade and the corruption it breeds as the greatest threat to the viability of a peaceful, democratic Afghan state. Afghan forces work side-by-side with U.S. and allied forces to combat terrorism and to fight the drug trade. The UK and United States both anticipate even greater cooperation in the fight against illicit drugs as we begin to implement an improved counter-narcotics strategy.

Questions for the Record Submitted to
Assistant Secretary Robert Charles by
Chairman Mark E. Souder (#7)
Subcommittee for Criminal Justice,
Drug Policy & Human Resources
Committee on Government Reform
February 26, 2004

Question :

Warlords and other factional military leaders may not be willing to comply, conform or cede their power or forfeit their financial base stemming from poppy growth and opium transportation. What pressures or influences will be necessary to reduce their complicity?

Answer:

Poppy cultivation in Afghanistan breeds instability and corruption and serves as a resource base for remaining warlords. The government of Afghanistan recognizes the threat of the drug trade and is committed to reducing and eventually eliminating poppy cultivation. President Karzai has begun to confront the warlord problem, and some of the most powerful warlords have seen their influence decrease in recent months. For counternarcotics efforts to be successful in Afghanistan, there must be an integrated strategy of interdiction against drug producers and traffickers, poppy crop eradication, alternative livelihood programs offering farmers legal ways of prospering, and assistance efforts building up the institutional capabilities of the Afghan police and judicial system. Persistent central government efforts in counternarcotics – strongly assisted and reinforced by the United States, the United Kingdom and other donors – will increasingly help to induce the warlords to comply with Afghanistan's anti-drug laws and policies.

Questions for the Record Submitted to
Assistant Secretary Robert Charles by
Chairman Mark E. Souder(#8)
Subcommittee for Criminal Justice,
Drug Policy & Human Resources
Committee on Government Reform
February 26, 2004

Question:

What connection do you see between poppy cultivation and transshipment and the remnants of the Taliban, Al Queda and or the war lords? Is the connection strong enough to implement a counter strategy? What strategy would you recommend? What is the evidence that terrorists are linked to narco-trafficking?

Answer:

Poppy cultivation, drug production and drug trafficking offer potential sources of illicit earnings to remnants of the Taliban, al-Qa'ida and warlords in Afghanistan. Remnants of the Taliban and various warlords appear to be recipients of illicit earnings from the drug trade.

We have anecdotal reports of drug trafficking by elements aligned with al-Qa'ida, but there is no corroborated information that drug trafficking provides a significant source of income for al-Qa'ida. The involvement of anti-government Afghan extremists in the drug trade is clearer: US troops in 2002 raided a heroin lab in Nangarhar Province linked to the Hizb-I Islami Gulbuddin and officials from the UN and the Afghan Government report that the Taliban earns money from the heroin trade. I recommend you contact the Drug Enforcement Administration and the Intelligence Community for more information on this topic.

Our counternarcotics strategy aims at depriving terrorists, criminals and anti-Coalition elements of the earnings from the poppy trade by reducing the amount of poppy cultivation and reducing the benefits and increasing the risks of the poppy trade to those involved in production, manufacturing and trafficking. INL's strategy is to work closely with the government of Afghanistan and coordinate with key allies who share our anti-drug objectives.

Questions for the Record Submitted to
Assistant Secretary Robert Charles by
Chairman Mark E. Souder (#9)
Subcommittee for Criminal Justice,
Drug Policy & Human Resources
Committee on Government Reform
February 26, 2004

Question:

In the most densely cultivated poppy fields, near rivers, for example, is there any possibility of using aerial eradication either with herbicides similar to those used in the Andean Region or using mycoherbicides?

Answer:

Given the conditions in Afghanistan and funding assistance levels, our plan has been to initiate poppy crop eradication using manual means. This approach does not exclude the possibility of aerial eradication at a later stage depending on the progress of manual eradication and lessons learned in implementing that approach. Two main challenges confronting a future aerial eradication program include developing the necessary infrastructure and acquiring air assets. While both challenges could be overcome, they will require a solid commitment and careful planning. The development of mycoherbicides remains at too early a stage of research for us to speculate at this time on the possibility of its use in Afghanistan.

Questions for the Record Submitted to
Assistant Secretary Robert Charles by
Chairman Mark E. Souder (#10)
Subcommittee for Criminal Justice,
Drug Policy & Human Resources
Committee on Government Reform
February 26, 2004

Question:

When the Pakistani government requested air mobility along the Afghan border, why did the State Department give the helicopters to the Ministry of Interior rather than the Pakistani Anti-Narcotics Force?

Answer:

Immediately after the September 11, 2001, terrorist attacks, INL received $73 million in Supplemental funding for a border security program to address security concerns along the Pakistan-Afghanistan frontier. The overall goal for this program is to enhance mobility and communications for the multiple agencies responsible for operations along the frontiers of Balochistan and North West Frontier Provinces, enabling them to improve interdiction of terrorists and traffickers in drugs, small arms, contraband, or persons.

While combating narcotics is one of the primary objectives of the program, improving Pakistan's capacity to interdict the movements of al-Qa'ida and Taliban remnants is another top priority for the program.

The program included procurement and deployment of an initial mix of aircraft (three fixed wing and five helicopters) that would serve as both surveillance platforms and means of tactical support for a rapid interdiction force. INL worked with the Government of Pakistan to choose an entity that could serve as an appropriate broker between the different priorities and provide support to multiple law enforcement agencies with differing missions. The Ministry of the Interior was chosen due to its ability to manage both priorities.

Questions for the Record Submitted to
Assistant Secretary Robert Charles by
Chairman Mark E. Souder (#11)
Subcommittee for Criminal Justice,
Drug Policy & Human Resources
Committee on Government Reform
February 26, 2004

Question:

The Afghanistan-Pakistan border is porous, with some tribes straddling both sides, making interdiction of narcotics complicated at best. How is the State Department working with the Pakistani government to clarify and deepen the level of cooperation between the Army, the Anti-Narcotics Force, the Frontier Corps, and the national police?

Answer:

INL funds are being used to improve the capacities of all civilian Pakistani agencies with counter-drug responsibilities – from federal entities like the Anti-Narcotics Force (ANF), Customs, and Frontier Corps to provincial police personnel. This assistance takes the form of vehicles, communications, and surveillance equipment; access to Ministry of Interior Air Wing assets (for those agencies operating on the western border); operational support for ANF; and training. Whenever feasible, training is conducted on an interagency basis to assist in building trust and compatible skills among the various law enforcement agencies.

INL is also working to overcome institutional rivalries and to promote the most effective use of the Ministry of Interior air assets and other commodities by promoting cooperation among the Frontier Corps, ANF, and the Ministry of Interior to establish a border security coordination center in Quetta. The center would integrate intelligence collection and analysis, as well as operational planning, for counter-narcotics and other border security missions.

The U.S. Embassy in Islamabad will also be working closely with the newly appointed Minister for Narcotics Control to develop interagency counter-trafficking cooperation; akin to the interagency cooperation we have promoted successfully to address opium poppy cultivation inside Pakistan.

Afghan Extremists' Links to the Drug Trade

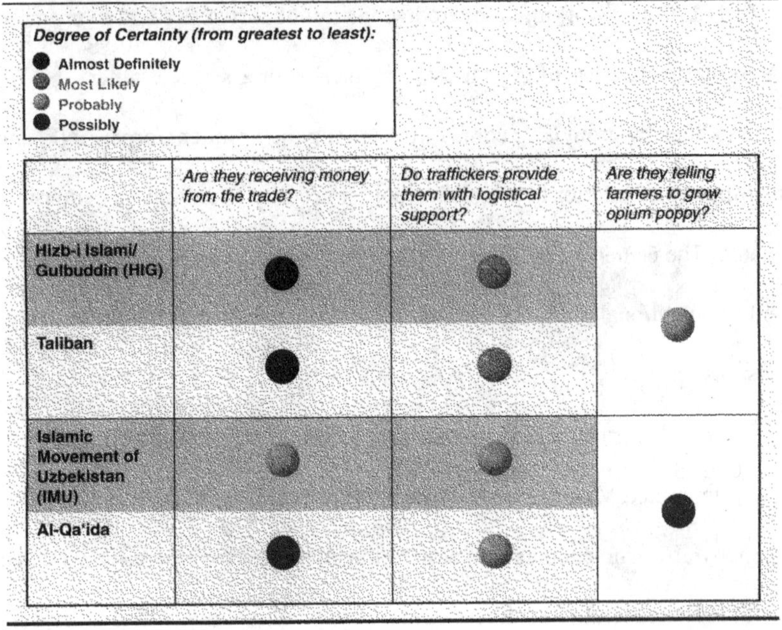

Afghan Extremists' Links to the Drug Trade

Degree of Certainty (from greatest to least):

Almost Definitely
Most Likely
Probably
Possibly

	Are they receiving money from the trade?	*Do traffickers provide them with logistical support?*	*Are they telling farmers to grow opium poppy?*
Hizb-I Islami/ Gulbuddin (HIG)	**Almost Definitely:** HIG commanders involved in trafficking have led attacks on Coalition forces, and US troops have raided heroin labs linked to the HIG.	**Most Likely:** HIG commanders involved in the drug trade may use those ties to facilitate weapons smuggling and money laundering.	**Probably:** Afghan Transitional Authority officials say the Taliban now encourages poppy cultivation, and other extremist groups interested in weakening the government in Kabul—like the HIG—may be following its lead.
Taliban	**Almost Definitely:** UN and Afghan Transitional Authority officials report the group earns money from trafficking and gets donations from drug lords.	**Most Likely:** Major drug barons who supported the Taliban when it was in power remain at large, and may be moving people, equipment, and money on the group's behalf.	
Islamic Movement of Uzbekistan (IMU)	**Probably:** Uzbekistani officials have accused the group of involvement in the drug trade, and its remnants in Afghanistan may turn to trafficking to raise funds.	**Probably:** Members with drug ties may turn to traffickers for help crossing borders.	**Possibly:** No reports, and these groups—as foreigners in Afghanistan—may lack the moral and political authority needed to influence farmers' planting decisions.
Al-Qa'ida	**Possibly:** Only scattered reports, but fighters in Afghanistan may be engaged in low-level—but still lucrative—drug deals.	**Probably:** Traffickers stopped last December in the Arabian Sea were linked to al-Qa'ida. Al-Qa'ida may hire professional criminals in South Asia to transfer its weapons, explosives, money, and people through the region.	

Southwest Asian Drug Flows

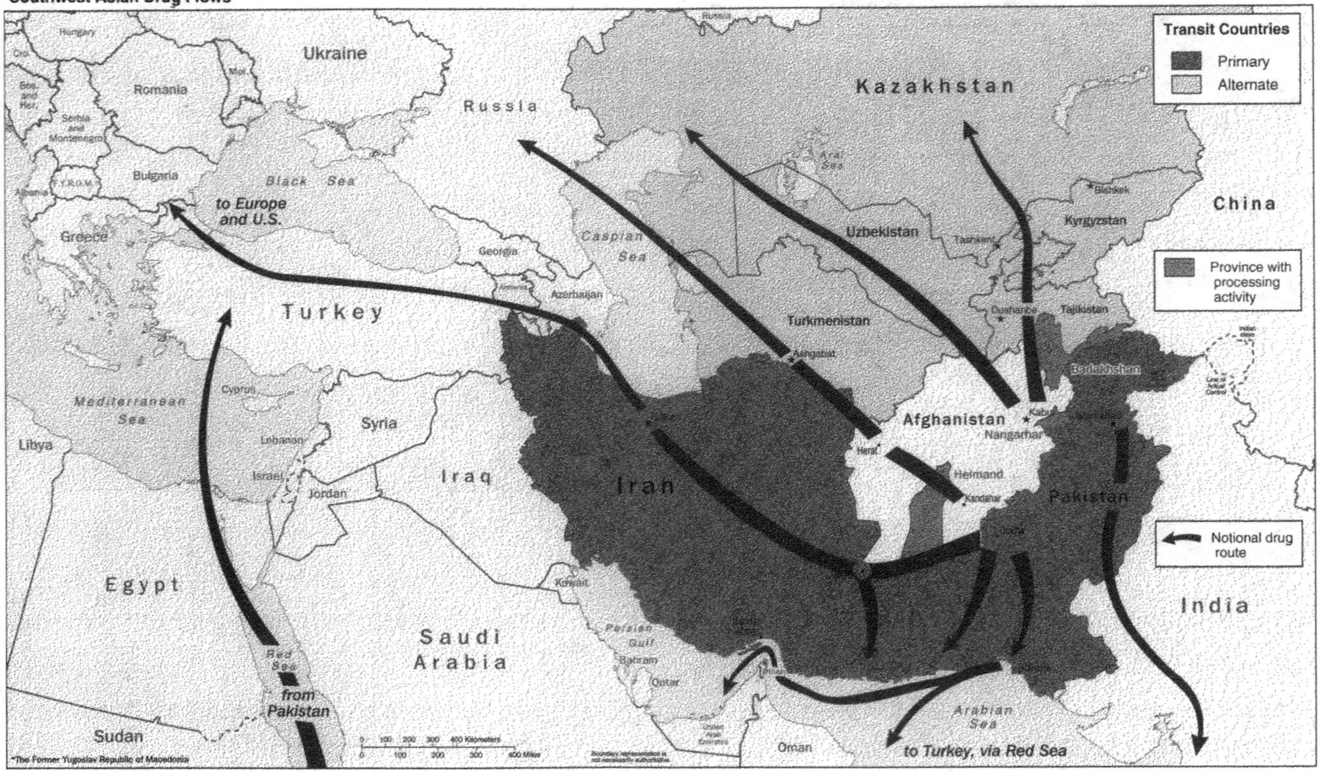

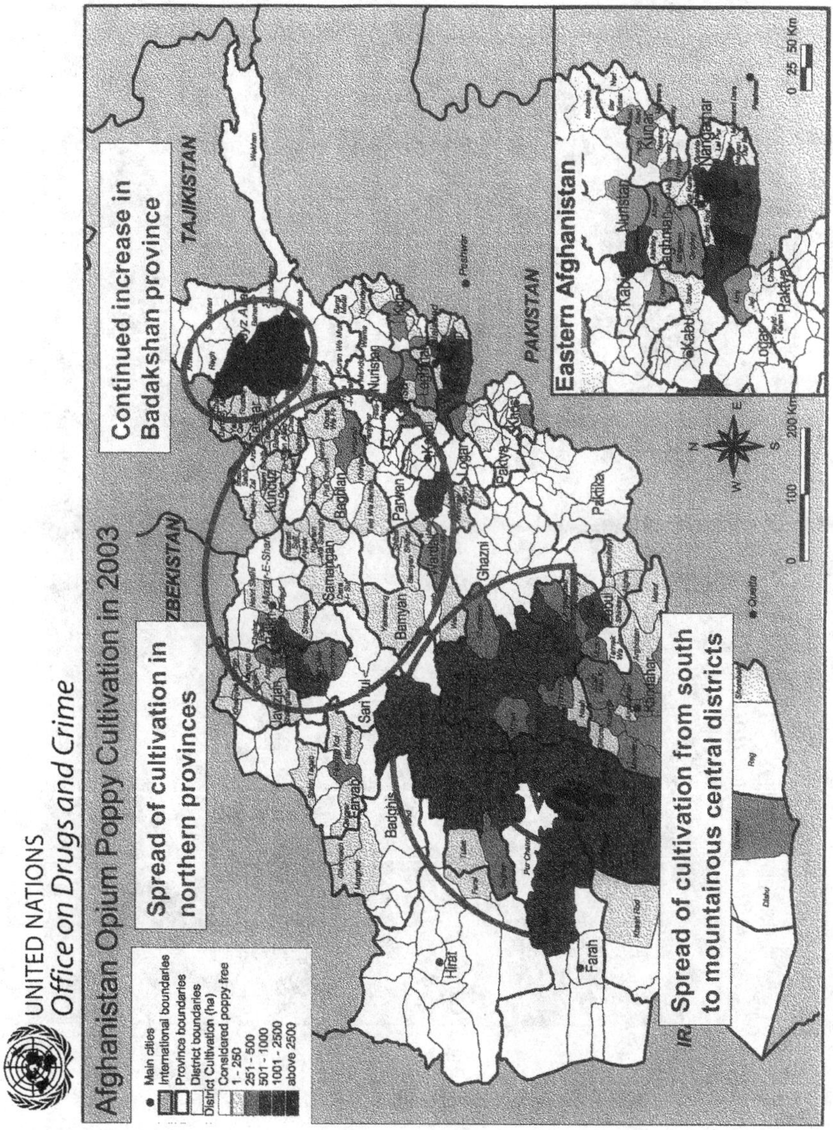

UNITED NATIONS
Office on Drugs and Crime
Afghanistan Opium Poppy Cultivation in 2003
Main cities
International boundaries
Province boundaries
District boundaries
District Cultivation (ha)
Considered poppy free
1 - 250
251 - 500
501 - 1000
1001 - 2500
above 2500
Spread of cultivation in northern provinces
Continued increase in Badakshan province
Spread of cultivation from south to mountainous central districts
Eastern Afghanistan
TAJIKISTAN
UZBEKISTAN
PAKISTAN
0 100 200 Km
0 25 50 Km

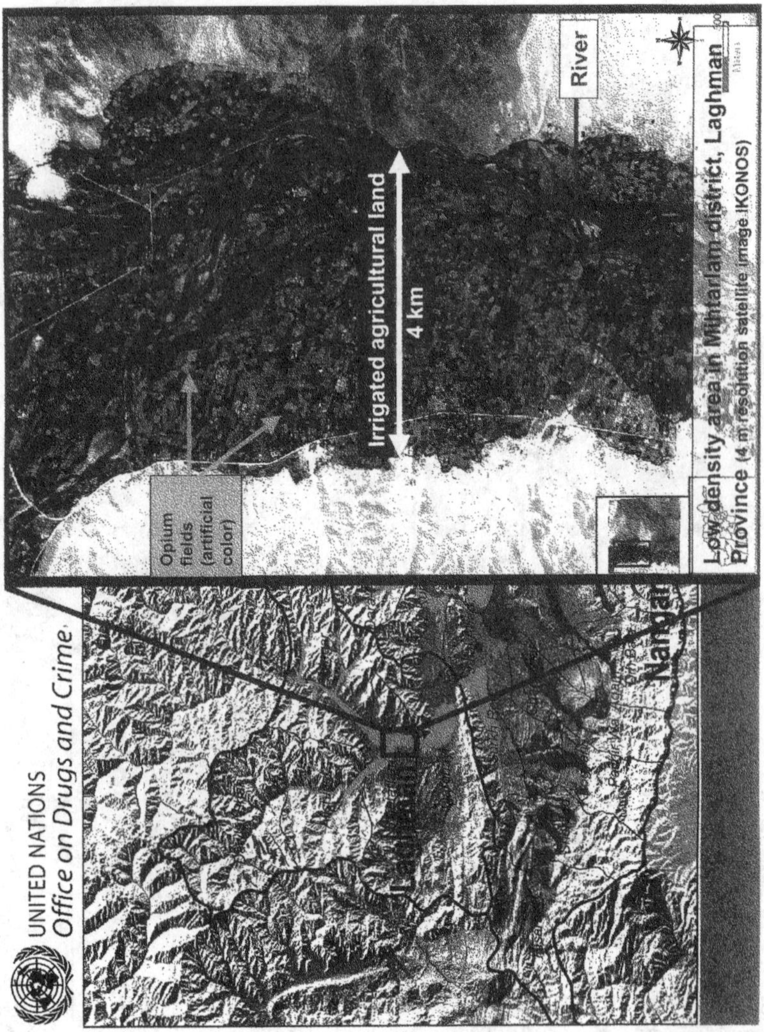
UNITED NATIONS
Office on Drugs and Crime
Opium fields (artificial color)
Irrigated agricultural land
4 km
River
Low density area in Mihtarlam district, Laghman Province (4 m resolution satellite image IKONOS)

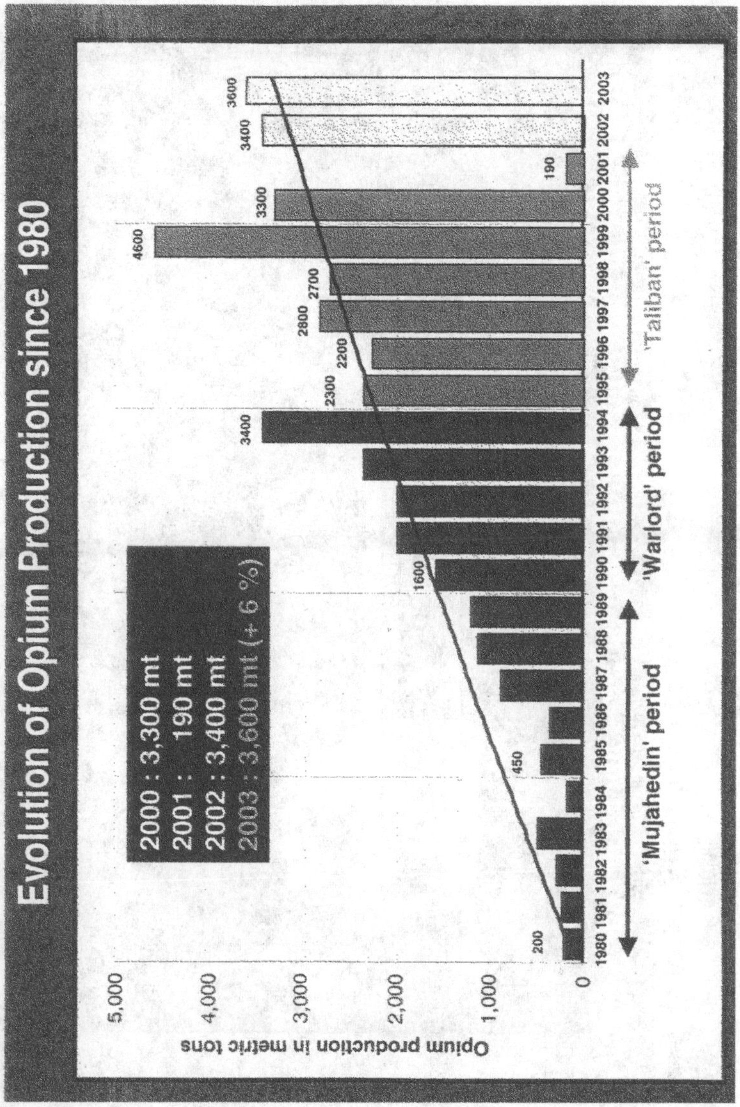
UNITED NATIONS
Office on Drugs and Crime
Evolution of Opium Production since 1980
2000 : 3,300 mt
2001 : 190 mt
2002 : 3,400 mt
2003 : 3,600 mt (+ 6 %)
Opium production in metric tons
5,000
4,000
3,000
2,000
1,000
0
200
450
1600
3400
2300
2200
2800
2700
4600
3300
190
3400
3600
1980 1981 1982 1983 1984 1985 1986 1987 1988 1989 1990 1991 1992 1993 1994 1995 1996 1997 1998 1999 2000 2001 2002 2003
'Mujahedin' period
'Warlord' period
'Taliban' period

UNITED NATIONS
Office on Drugs and Crime

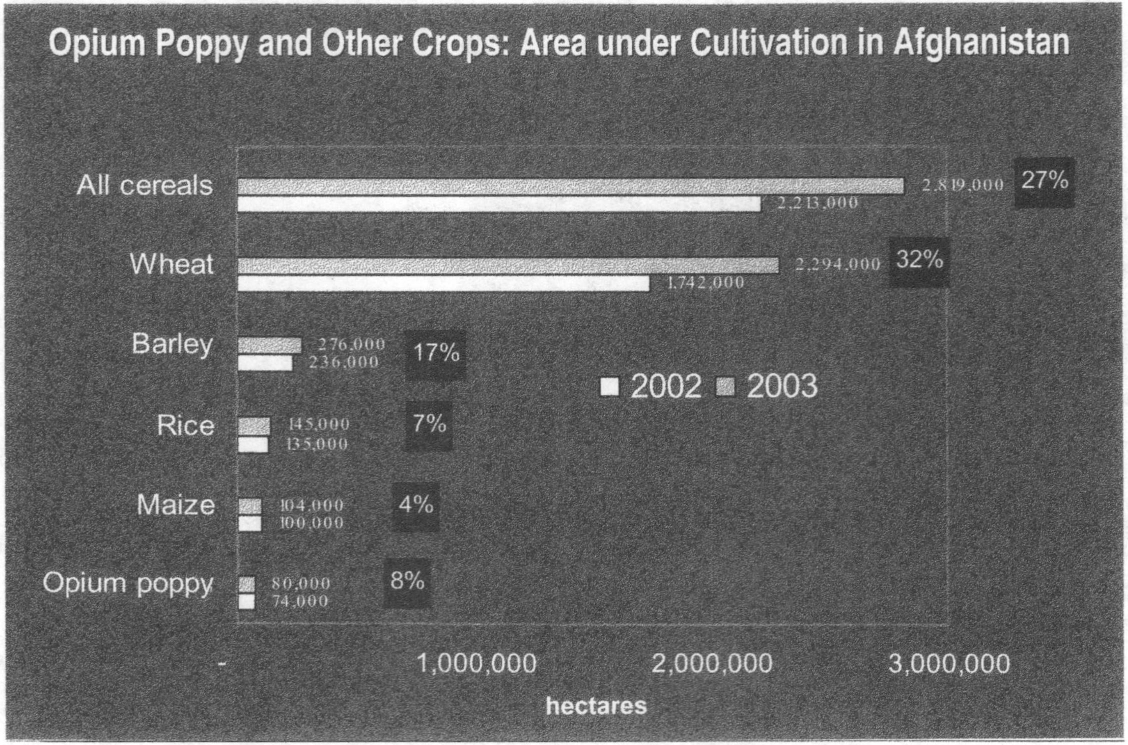

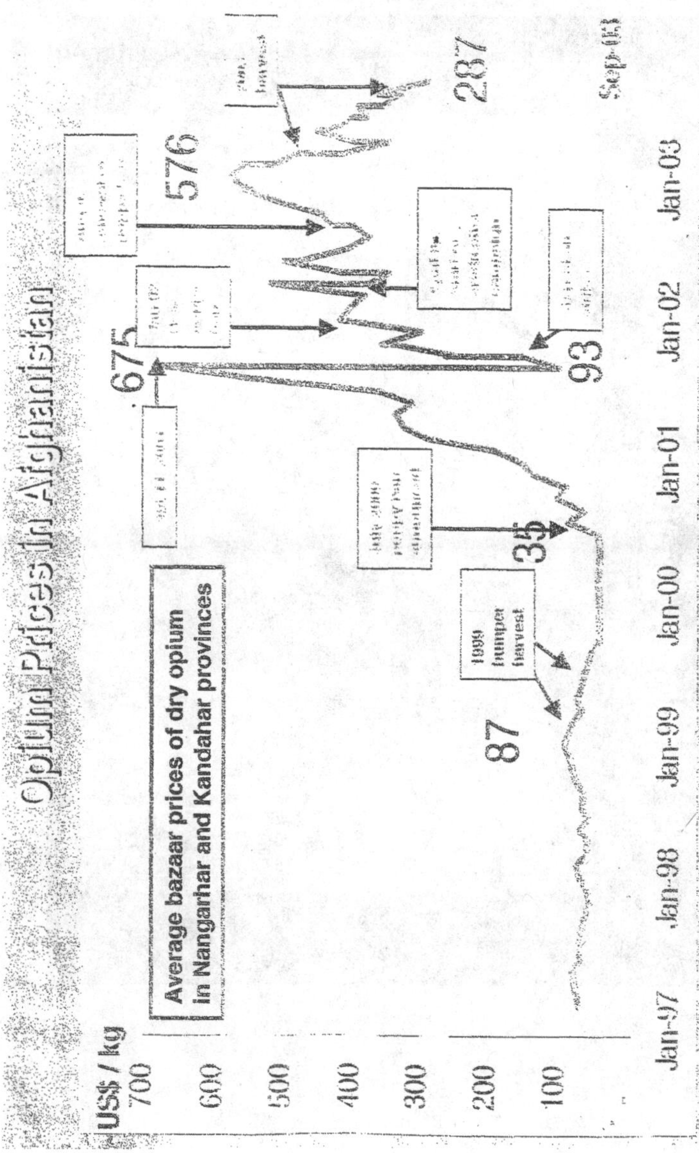
Opium Prices in Afghanistan
Average bazaar prices of dry opium
in Nangarhar and Kandahar provinces
US$ / kg
700
600
500
400
300
200
100
Jan-97
Jan-98
Jan-99
Jan-00
Jan-01
Jan-02
Jan-03
Sep-03
87
1999 bumper harvest
35
675
93
576
287
harvest

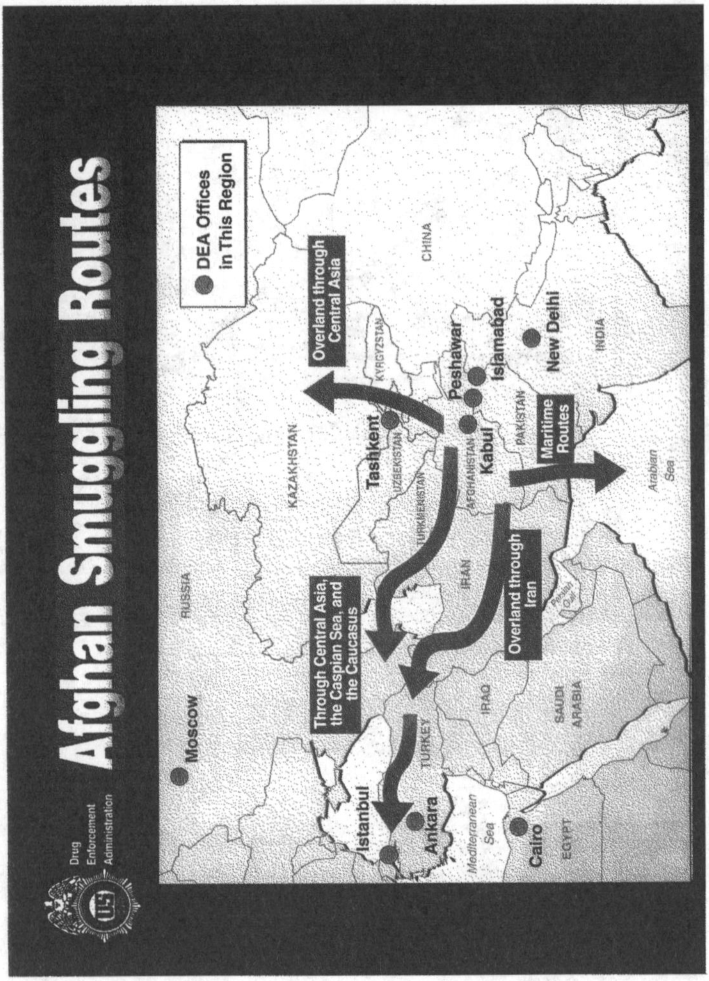
Drug
Enforcement
Administration
Afghan Smuggling Routes
DEA Offices in This Region
Overland through Central Asia
Through Central Asia, the Caspian Sea, and the Caucasus
Overland through Iran
Maritime Routes
Moscow
RUSSIA
KAZAKHSTAN
CHINA
KYRGYZSTAN
UZBEKISTAN
TURKMENISTAN
AFGHANISTAN
PAKISTAN
INDIA
IRAN
IRAQ
TURKEY
SAUDI ARABIA
EGYPT
Tashkent
Kabul
Peshawar
Islamabad
New Delhi
Istanbul
Ankara
Cairo
Mediterranean Sea
Arabian Sea
Persian Gulf